REAL ESTATE INVESTMENT

How to Double Your Money Every Two to Three Years

KENNETH KIMMEL

CORNERSTONE LIBRARY
NEW YORK

Copyright © 1980 by Kenneth M. Kimmel

All rights reserved, including the right of reproduction
in whole or in part, in any form

Published by Cornerstone Library
A Simon & Schuster Subsidiary of
Gulf & Western Corporation
Simon & Schuster Building
1230 Avenue of the Americas
New York, New York 10020

The trademark of Cornerstone Library, Inc. consists of the words
"Cornerstone Library" and the portrayal of a cube and is registered
in the United States Patent Office

Manufactured in the United States of America

ISBN 346-12439-5

*To My Daughters
Julie and Emily*

CONTENTS

INTRODUCTION / xv

1 REAL ESTATE INVESTMENT 1

GETTING STARTED / 1
COMMON MYTHS ABOUT REAL ESTATE / 2
ESSENTIAL INVESTMENT CONCEPTS / 3
   Profitable Acquisition / 4
   Cash Flow / 6
   Equity Growth / 8
   Tax Shelter / 11
   Total Yield / 16
   Individual Investment Goals / 18
   Risk Factors and General Economic Trends / 19
   Inflation / 21
   Liquidity / 22
   Leverage / 24

2 Single-Family Dwellings 28

REVERSING URBAN BLIGHT / 30
A "CORNER" ON THE HOUSING MARKET / 30
ACQUIRING THE SINGLE FAMILY DWELLING / 32
SIMPLE CONVERSION—HIGH RETURN / 37

MANAGEMENT / 38
MAINTENANCE / 43

3 Multiple-Family Dwellings — 47

SIMILARITIES BETWEEN SINGLE AND MULTIPLE FAMILY RENTAL UNITS / 49
DISTINCTIONS BETWEEN SINGLE AND MULTIPLE FAMILY RENTAL UNITS / 49
LARGER COMPLEXES / 52
DEGREE OF FINANCIAL ENCUMBRANCE / 52
DEGREE OF MANAGEMENT AND MAINTENANCE / 53
POSSIBLE JOINT OWNERSHIP, TRUSTS / 54
DIVERSITY OF AMENITIES / 55
CLOSER ASSOCIATION WITH SUPPORT PROFESSIONALS / 56
QUALITY OF INCOME AND DEGREE OF TAX SHELTER / 57
CONDOMINIUMS / 58
COOPERATIVES / 59

4 Land, Commercial, Industrial & Recreational properties — 61

LAND / 61
COMMERCIAL PROPERTY / 67
MOTELS / 71
INDUSTRIAL PROPERTY / 74
RECREATIONAL PROPERTY / 76

5 How To Accurately Assess The Value of A Property — 80

ANALYSIS OF THE ASKING PRICE, SELLER'S MOTIVATION, AND THE ORIGINAL ACQUISITION PRICE / 81
ONE MORE FOOL THEORY / 82

ANALYSIS AND JUSTIFICATION FOR CURRENT AND
   PREVIOUS TAX ASSESSMENT / 83
ANALYSIS OF TOTAL INCOME VS. TOTAL EXPENSES / 84
ANALYSIS OF SQUARE FOOTAGE AND ADDITIONAL
   AMENITIES / 85
ANALYSIS OF LOCATION, VISUAL APPEAL AND
   DESIRABILITY / 89
ANALYSIS OF COMPARABLE VALUES AND/OR SALES / 91
ANALYSIS OF BROAD ECONOMIC FACTORS / 92
ANALYSIS OF TERMS RELATIVE TO COST AND RATE OF
   PROJECTED RETURN / 94
ANALYSIS OF BUYER MOTIVATION, NEEDS AND
   CAPABILITIES / 96

6 Buying Income-Producing Property at the Best Price   98

INVESTOR'S INITIAL INQUIRY FORM / 99
  Date / 101
  Address of Property For Sale / 101
  Directions on How to Find / 102
  Complete Description as advertised, asking price, and
    Source of Information / 102
  Seller's name, address and telephone / 103
  Seller's Agent (Name, Address and Telephone) / 104
  Stated Reason for Selling / 105
  Evaluation of neighborhood / 105
  Legal Description / 107
  Total Square Footage of the Building / 108
  Total Square Footage of the Lot / 109
  County's Assessed Value and Taxes Paid Last Year / 111
  Financial Terms Desired / 112
  Notes / 113
SELLER'S SUMMARY OF PROPERTY CONDITION AND
   EXPENSES / 114

7 Conventional and Creative Methods of Financing Real Estate — 117

CONVENTIONAL FINANCING / 117
FEDERAL FINANCING / 118
STATE FINANCING / 119
PRIVATE FINANCING / 120
BUYING AND SELLING ON CONTRACT / 122
ADVANTAGES FOR THE CONTRACT BUYER / 124
THE DIRECT APPROACH / 124
VALUE OF A CONTRACT FROM THE SELLER'S POINT OF VIEW / 126
DEVELOPING AND FINANCING A LARGE APARTMENT COMPLEX / 130
VARIATIONS ON THE "NO-MONEY-DOWN" THEME / 132
ACQUIRE A $100,000 ASSET WITH NO MONEY DOWN / 134
HIGH-PERCENTAGE DOWN PAYMENTS / 134

8 Tenant Selection For Maximum Profit and Minimum Headache — 137

STARTING RIGHT OFF / 137
AVOID THE BIG MISTAKES / 138
MINIMIZE PROSPECTS WHO "WANT TO LOOK AROUND" / 139
THE REQUIRED WRITTEN APPLICATION / 140
APPLICATION FOR RENTAL / 141
VERIFICATION OF FINANCIAL REFERENCES / 143
VERIFICATION OF STATED INCOME / 144
RULE OF FOUR-TO-ONE / 145
VERIFICATION OF FORMER RENTAL HISTORY / 146
VERIFICATION OF PERSONAL REFERENCES / 146
SAMPLE RENTAL AGREEMENT / 147

THE MOVE-IN CHECKLIST / 148
AVOIDING LATE RENT PAYMENTS / 149
TENANT RIGHTS / 150
   Minimum Housing Quality Standards / 151
   Contract Law / 152
   Rent Control Regulations / 153
   Anti-Discrimination Laws / 153
   Avoiding Tenant Eviction / 155

9 Rental-Property Maintenance and General Management   160

PREVENTATIVE MAINTENANCE / 167
THE IMPORTANCE OF PAINT / 169
MAINTENANCE BEGINS BEFORE YOU BUY / 172
IMPORTANCE OF CREATIVE LANDSCAPING / 174
NO PETS ALLOWED / 176
SAMPLE CHECKLIST OF THE 12 POTENTIAL
   MAINTENANCE PROBLEMS / 177

10 Creative Ways to Sell or Exchange Income-Producing Properties   179

DIRECT OR INSTALLMENT SALE / 180
REFINANCE / 182
TAX-DEFERRED EXCHANGES / 185
SELECTING YOUR PERSONAL REAL ESTATE BROKER / 192
GLOSSARY / 197

INDEX / 213

INTRODUCTION

This book is devoted to the methods of attaining total financial independence (creation of wealth, if you insist) through the methodical and conservative handling of income-producing properties. This book will not be especially helpful for the individual who wants to know "How to Make $1,000,000 in Real Estate Starting from Scratch in Three Years or Less!" Numerous writers have documented the fact that such statistically rare events have occurred. So what! A more tangible statistical fact that will be relevant for virtually everyone who may use this instructional book is that 90% to 95% of the persons over age 65 in this country are *not* totally financially independent! Only one person out of every ten to twenty persons over 65 years of age is totally self-supporting, without dependence upon social welfare programs such as social security, pension plans, public welfare, or mandatory continued employment. The often bitter realities of continuous, compounding inflation is making such programs obsolete. Taxable savings accounts paying 5% annual interest are a joke. The standard of living of all persons dependent upon salaries-only and/or social welfare programs is declining. With inflation compounded annually at 10%, today's $5,000 economy car will cost $11,790 in 1988, and that same car in the year 2008 will cost $73,805! Your current sacrifices to contribute to that pension plan could be largely in vain. Want to do something about it? Start here. Read. Compare. Utilize professional assistance. Decide for yourself that methodical and conservative handling of income-producing property *is* the means for attaining total financial independence.

This book will deal with the basic concepts which are essential for success with income-producing investment properties. The information contained here is slanted toward the self-reliant individual who still "thinks" and one who has the self-confidence to occasionally challenge "conventional wisdom." This material should be of value to the novice investor, the sophisticated amateur, and the self-improvable professional. The novice with $1,000 to invest has as much opportunity to gain from this book as the person trying to invest $100,000 and more. In keeping with the title of this book, the basic theme is that the cautious beginner (novice) and certainly the experienced professional can make a "total yield"* of 35% to 50% (and more!) on their original investment—each and every year! For the individuals who are determined to set $1,000,000 as their personal goal, all they have to do is start with $1,000 and reliably double their money ten times ($1,000^{10} = $1,000,000). The actual scale for becoming a millionaire would be as follows: $1,000, $2,000, $4,000, $8,000, $16,000, $32,000, $64,000, $128,000, $256,000, $512,000, and, finally, $1,024,000! The individual who starts with $8,000 and can reliably double that investment every two years would be a millionaire in fourteen years. With $32,000 to invest, the same process will take approximately ten years. Income-producing property is the only reliable "investment vehicle" with a strong enough performance record for novice and expert alike to double their initial investment *every* two to three years!

The source material for this book has been carefully gathered and shaped by the author's own "part-time" investment activities over the past twenty to twenty-five years. This writer initially began the learning process by doing maintenance work for hometown real estate investors as an adolescent. After four years of college this "obsession" changed to apartment management with an "international" real estate firm to learn everything possible about management, tenant selection, legal matters, court-tested forms, general procedures, and problem resolution. During those early years, along with a routine government job, single-family dwellings were slowly acquired and converted to income-producing properties. In more recent years interests have been confined primarily to multiple-family residential complexes and related investment properties throughout the Pacific Northwest.

Wherever possible the scope of the material contained here has been broadened enough to be applicable on a nationwide, or broader, base. The basic contents of this book has been derived from countless investment seminars, investment books, articles, and library research (review of almost everything related to real estate investment—books, newsletters, journals, pamphlets, metropolitan newspapers), and recorded notes following years of intentional contacts with real estate brokers, buyers and sellers, government agencies, certified public accountants, attorneys, insurance agents, appraisors, property managers, I.R.S. auditors, contractors, tradesmen and laborers, bankers, miscellaneous vendors, tenants, county assessors and deed recorders, title company staff, various investors, and others. The accumulated value of the individual bits of information that have contributed to a workable strategy for learning to double your initial investment every two years would be immeasurably beyond the cost of this publication. Miscellaneous sources which have made a significant contribution to the investment philosophy of this book include Boston: "Real Estate Investor Letter," The Lowry/Nickerson Seminar,* Huskin and Monsee's *How to Get Rich While You Sleep* (Cornerstone Library, New York, N.Y.), Mark Haroldsen's "Financial Freedom Library®," Stanley McMichael's

---

*Also see Albert Lowry's *How You Can Become Financially Independent by Investing in Real Estate* (Simon and Schuster, New York, N.Y., 1977); or William Nickerson's *How I Turned $1,000 into $3,000,000 in Real Estate—in My Spare Time* (Simon and Schuster, New York, N.Y., 1969).

How to Make Money in Real Estate (Prentice Hall, Englewood Cliffs, N.J.), Robert J. Ringer's *Winning Through Intimidation* (Fawcett, New York, N.Y.), Richard Reno's *Profitable Real Estate Exchanging and Counseling* (Prentice-Hall, Englewood Cliffs, N.J.), *U.S. Master Tax Guide,* "Tax Reform Act of 1976," "Revenue Act of 1978," George Fass, *The Fass System for Profits in Residential Income Property,* "Real Estate Review," published by The Real Estate Institute of New York University, *The Wall Street Journal, The New York Times, Los Angeles Times, Seattle Times,* and the hundreds of "ordinary" people across the country who have contributed to a financial independence philosophy that will work!

REAL ESTATE INVESTMENT

1

Real Estate Investment

GETTING STARTED

Real estate investment is not for everyone. Investment in income-producing properties is not the easiest, safest, or even the quickest medium of capital investment. Municipal bonds are easier. Well-secured, investment-quality, gems or gold bullion may be safer, and most retail goods offer a quicker return on the initial investment. The important distinction to be made is that at the end of one or more years even the best of "investments" in other areas will not compare favorably with well purchased and well managed income-producing properties. No other tangible asset has the unique combination of persistent demand, high leverage, minimum risk, protection of ownership, appreciation, tax shelter, inflation hedge, and potential to generate reliable income as the well-purchased and well-managed income-producing property! All of these claims are subject to verification, and you are respectfully invited to do so. Be skeptical. Begin your investment career by personally validating the often hysterical claims and promises that are made about real estate investment. Success in meeting personal goals as an investor usually accompanies the individual who approaches each situation in a critically thoughtful manner and one who remains flexible to changing circumstances. Consider, for example, three common myths about real estate that have been perpetuated to rationalize all manner of real estate investments—good and bad.

COMMON MYTHS ABOUT REAL ESTATE

1. There is only so much land and the population continues to increase.
2. Real estate will always go up in value.
3. Buy now because it will cost you more later.

Throughout the early and middle 1970s, the faulty premise and logic stated in the three steps above appeared to have an "ironclad" validity as land, private home values, and income-producing properties "inflated" in value at a staggering pace. Within a few years, and a few short-term buyers later, a private residential home which originally sold for $50,000 was being seriously marketed for $125,000! The situation was primarily hysterical. In Southern California, for instance, developers of tract homes (as opposed to custom homes) would announce the intention of a new development and either raffle off position numbers to wait in line to apply for the privilege of buying one of these tract houses, or, in other cases, the potential buyer would literally have to camp on the proposed site (a camper was often obtained for that very purpose) for a specified period of time to convince the realtors and developers involved of the "seriousness" of the intent of the prospective buyers! The incentive for the buyer was that the home which could be purchased prior to construction for $80,000 could be sold upon completion for more than $100,000! The result of such harsh, runaway economics has been an equally harsh Proposition 13 to alleviate the burden of the confiscatory property taxes. The housing market in Southern California has calmed down. Prices have remained high. The difference is that there has been an almost complete disappearance of buyers who will continue to pay even more. Discontented are the individuals who came in late and cannot afford to hold indefinitely without selling for a profit.

Real estate prices have always had periods of rising and falling. A different kind of example would be the severe recession that occurred for thousands of individuals in the Seattle area following massive layoffs at the Boeing Aircraft Company in the early 1970s. At that time there were large numbers of homes which could be acquired by assuming the existing mortgage! Families were desperate to get out because they simply could not afford the monthly payments. Large numbers of real estate offices and other businesses also went bankrupt during this time. Within a short time most real estate values had returned to their former levels. Currently the Pacific Northwest is experiencing an inflationary spiral similar to the one in California. Economic currents tend to change in subtle and mildly unpredictable manners. Riding an "inflationary wave" can be analogous to riding an ocean wave on a surfboard. With a measurable degree of skill and risk, the surfer is able to surge out ahead of the underlying currents. This delicate maneuver can be exhilarating and immensely rewarding. Most individuals continue to move around in the changing currents as if they didn't possess a surfboard, or didn't possess the same skills. Some are perhaps drowning. The "surfer" who tries to do too much too fast is subject to "going under." The distinction is that the individual who applies the basic skills will learn from mistakes and start over again if necessary, and with new assurance.

ESSENTIAL INVESTMENT CONCEPTS

Many things may be associated with real estate investment which could be of great significance to an individual investor. Concepts such as "pride of ownership," a sense of accomplishment, fantasies of the creation of wealth, or a desirable part-time or full-time career could be relevant topics for consideration in developing and pursuing an investment plan. This particular chapter will attempt to summarize what this writer considers the *basic* decision areas in formulating a conservative and highly

4 Real Estate Investment

profitable investment strategy. The five *most basic* elements in a lucrative real estate investment strategy are as follows:

1. Profitable Acquisition
2. Cash Flow (cash spendable)
3. Equity Growth (including appreciation)
4. Tax Shelter
5. Total Yield (including profits of sale)

Additional considerations which are generally a significant part of the decision to invest or *not* to invest in a particular property are as follows:

6. Individual Investment Goals
7. Risk Factors & General Economic Trends
8. Inflation
9. Liquidity
10. Leverage ("O.P.M.")

PROFITABLE ACQUISITION

Real estate agents and sellers often speak of cash flow, appreciation, and tax shelters with much enthusiasm to justify or at least mollify the effect of the typically "puffed-up" sales price. The figures cited to justify the sale price are based on future projections and under fairly idealistic conditions. A property that may be very profitable to the current owner (especially with a profitable sale) must now be demonstrated to be at least potentially profitable under the new financing and with projected gross rental income and gross expenses. The new financial circumstances can suddenly become a new reality which you must relate to in some fashion day after day until you exit from the investment. Upon acquisition of a new property, you will automatically establish a "basis," or perhaps transfer an existing "basis" into the new property. There will be a new debt service on the property, new responsibilities for maintenance and management, and new tax consequences for the buyer. Making such momentous decisions implies that certain risks and obligations must be assumed at the moment of acquisition.* Some complications, such as deferred maintenance, hidden expenses, and unexpected surprises (see Chapters 5 and 6 regarding assessment and buying), are inevitable and potentially expensive to resolve. Right up to the instant of signing that earnest money agreement (unless protected by an appropriate number of "subject to's," or "in lieu of's"**) a significant amount of attention must be devoted to analyzing favorable acquisitions and of rejecting inferior investments. Expressed another way, to make a conservative and financially successful investment, you *must* make your money "on the buy." In a "seller's market" this can mean paying the full asking price, with most of your effort going into schemes for obtaining the best possible terms, especially the most favorable interest rate obtainable, or lower down payment, etc. There are at least nine possibilities in calculating price and terms alone!

1. Good terms—Good price—Most desirable
2. Good terms—Fair Price— Desirable
3. Good terms—Poor Price— Occasionally desirable
4. Fair terms— Good price—Desirable
5. Fair terms— Fair price— Potentially desirable
6. Fair terms— Poor price— Undesirable (avoid)
7. Poor terms— Good price—Potentially desirable
8. Poor terms— Fair price— Undesirable (be extra careful)
9. Poor terms— Poor price— Most undesirable (forget it!)

The creative and well-timed manipulation of "terms" is probably the best tool a buyer has in a highly competitive and rapidly appreciating market. A buyer who is thorough and assertive about an investment plan should not have a great reluctance to offer a three-, four-, or five-year equity payoff (technically a refinance if the property has not been sold or exchanged during that interval) to the installment seller, who must avoid excessive capital gains tax, yet does not want a long-term (same as low-return) contract. Interest rates are another condition that can

---
*Technically, the obligation can begin at the critical moment of first commitment, or signature on a "binding" contract.
**See Chapter 6 on buying, especially when and how to negotiate your offer.

almost always be negotiated downward *in the final minutes before* signing the earnest money agreement. The reduction may be only a fraction of one percent, but it's worth fighting for. Interest reductions are much more likely when the seller is genuinely intent upon selling and especially where intermediaries are not involved. Another term that can be altered on contract sales is the waiver of all principle payments for a specified period of time.* Dates of acquisition can be creatively timed. Controls such as allowances for various inspections, verifications, or possible warranties can be used as effective bargaining tools (once you've progressed to the point where you are confident that you want to buy and seller wants to sell**). In summary, profits in real estate can be more readily obtained by developing good financing opportunities than by adhering strictly to the "buy low and sell high" procedure.

CASH FLOW

Cash flow is a major component of the decision to accept or reject a particular investment property. It is a commonly abused concept and therefore should be carefully analyzed before allowing a "positive" or "negative" cash flow to influence your decision about a particular investment. Simply stated, a cash flow is the monthly balance from a given income property after subtracting all monthly expenses and the debt service from the total monthly income. This is part of the "spendable" and therefore "taxable" income that will occur on a monthly basis. The cash flow for a particular month could hypothetically be zero. In reality it will likely be a surplus (positive cash flow) or a deficit (negative cash flow). The following would be a typical example of positive cash flow:

---

*It is not "legal" for mutual savings banks or other commercial lenders to approve loans which are not self-amortizing.
**A specially good reference on this particular topic would be Robert J. Ringer's best-selling book on the arts of negotiation and related facts, titled *Winning Through Intimidation* (Fawcett, New York, N.Y., 1979).

HILL VILLA APARTMENTS (5-Plex)

INCOME
Gross annual income (275/mo.) $16,500

DEBT SERVICE
Purchase price was $125,000 with   9,500 (interest)
20% down ($25,000) & balance of   700 (equity)
$100,000 @ 9.5% (30 yrs.) or 850/mo. $10,200

EXPENSES
Exterior electricity	$ 200
Fire and liability insurance	300
Maintenance (5% of gross)	825
Management	300
Misc. (advertising, fees, signs)	100
Property taxes (1½% market value)	1,875
Vacancy & collection loss (2% of gross)	330
Water, sewer, and garbage	300

CASH FLOW: ($16,500 minus $10,200 + $4,230) = $2,070

"Cash on Cash" = cash flow divided by down payment, or $\dfrac{\$2,070}{\$25,000} = 8\%$

A property which is "overfinanced" or raw land would be typical situations that would result in a negative cash flow. The total cash paid out exceeds the total cash paid in. Gross discrepancies in this area (often referred to as a "big alligator") can result in financial disaster. As a concept in either buying or selling income-producing property, "cash flow" is generally represented as an annual figure. Having a consistent positive cash flow is primarily a function of the quality of the net income as compared to the amount paid down. Newer, attractive multiples which are purchased with approximately 10% to 15% down will invariably produce a negative or "reverse" cash flow. Under such circumstances it is especially important to accurately analyze the quality and variability of the gross scheduled rents, expenses, vacancies, collection losses, and regional economic trends. It is true that you can profit from a negative cash flow situation through exceptionally high tax shelter and the "roulette wheel of fortune" if appreciation is driven upward by the continued high rate of inflation. In a negative cash flow situation, the investor must make up the month-to-month differences between total income and total expenses from some other source ("out-of-pocket monies"). Having the financial strength to preserve the investment without drastic over-reactions can be critical. Properties with a good "annual" cash flow often have bad months when all expenses seem to come together, such as insurance premiums, heating bills, unexpected repairs, a slump in the percent of occupancy, and possible collection losses. The best resolution for such "shocks" to your monthly budget is to carefully analyze variable expenses in advance, and where possible arrange for monthly averaging of expenses with certain vendors (especially fuel companies, or electrical companies, where heat may be furnished). Make insurance premiums payable, and make major repairs, at less critical times of the year. Give special attention to upgrading the credit quality of the tenants when possible, and likewise, give special attention to the quality of service provided for the tenants. Anticipate, manage, and be prepared to resolve needs quickly. Carefully chosen tenants whose basic concerns are attended to can be the equivalent of a positive cash flow.

EQUITY GROWTH

Equity growth, when narrowly defined as the month-to-month principle gain, is the least significant return on most real estate investments. Frequently contracts of sale between private parties will allow for interest-only payments and a waiver of any principle payments! In the early years of a conventional loan, the principle (equity growth) represents less than 6% to 8% of the total interest and principle payment. The broader definition of equity growth is the one that is most commonly referred to by investors. That is, excluding the initial cost of acquisition, equity growth is any month-to-month principle gain *and* the assumed change in value as a result of increased rents, appreciation, and physical upgrading. This is generally expressed as being the "current market equity" or "list price equity."

Recent history has demonstrated that real property equities can actually decline in value. Major cities throughout the United States have continually had highly visible examples of multistory office buildings, condominiums, and other high-rise units that are virtually vacant months and years after completion. The inevitable consequence is that a loss is eventually taken on the building. "Abandoned" buildings are commonplace in New York City, where there has been a steady exodus of businesses and employees due to severe taxes, technological displacements, problems in raising sufficient revenues, rent control, and basic economics such as private lenders staying away from New York City rental housing, and decline of investor interest as risks escalate. The unfortunate decade of the 1930s was a classic example of overwhelming numbers of property loans which went into default because of declines in value and the inability to meet minimum interest and property tax payments. In such cases the banks generally called in the loans in which the borrower had an equity of 50% or more. The borrowers with "thin" equities were often allowed to work out other means of eventual payment. The distinction was that the banks could "profitably" unload the high-equity properties despite the big discounts. The chances of having another chronic economic decline such as in the Thirties are quite remote. As in the Thirties, the chances that a specific individual can experience a chronic economic decline are very real. Investors, even persons who "lose it all," are likely to be perceptive to drastic economic changes and utilize that information to "make it all back!" Most investors will do better than "survive." It is the non-investors who are being "robbed" of their current standard of living.

The components that make up the concept of equity growth are subject to possible misinterpretation. The original down payment is the *only* component of equity growth at the time of closing a transaction. Within one to five years the original down payment may represent only a small percentage of the current market equity. And despite this rapidly changing significance, many investors continue to evaluate the success of their investment by the amount of gain relative to the initial down payment. In the first couple of years or so, it may be reasonably accurate to compare the percentage of annual return with the original investment. After the fourth or fifth year the accumulation of equity as a result of upgrading, appreciation, and principle payments can significantly distort your perception of the true annual return on a particular investment. Example: in 1971 an older six-plex was purchased on contract for $50,000 with 20% down, or $10,000. The "return on the initial investment" was always satisfactory, and the owner was completely unaware of the potential income being lost! The rate of return was as follows:

Year	Property Value	Mortgage Balance	Equity Growth	Cash Flow	Return on $10,000	Return on Eq. Growth
1971	50,000	40,000	10,000	1,400	.14	.14
1972	52,500	39,488	13,012	1,500	.15	.12
1973	55,125	38,983	16,142	1,560	.16	.10
1974	57,881	38,437	19,444	1,624	.16	.08
1975	62,511	37,880	24,631	1,740	.17	.07
1976	66,887	37,274	29,613	1,880	.19	.06
1977	72,238	36,640	35,598	1,975	.20	.06
1978	78,739	35,999	42,740	2,210	.22	.05

Before the end of the third year a significant turning point had been reached. Despite a firm and modestly increasing cash flow, the return on the accumulated equity began to reach unfavorable levels. In 1973 this investor could have converted approximately $16,000 in equity growth into an $80,000-to-$100,000 investment property and repeat the early steps of the above process at a significantly higher level. It is rarely correct to just "sit" on an investment property. Other options include refinance, creative sale, or exchange.

TAX SHELTER

The economic factor which distinguishes income-producing properties from virtually all other forms of investment is the capability to create "tax shelter." The less provocative term for essentially the same thing is "depreciation." It is through depreciation that a loss on paper can be transformed into a gain in terms of real income. Newly constructed apartments would rarely show a profit, and the "incentive" to risk personal capital and assume the "passive" responsibilities of income-property ownership and management would hardly exist without the allowances for depreciation. The income-property investor is obligated to be knowledgeable about the general details of various methods of computing depreciation. The specific details as they may apply to a particular situation should be left to your personal accountant or tax attorney for interpretation of refinements within the law, I.R.S. "guidelines," and to assist you in being arithmetically accurate. Sloppiness in the computation of depreciation schedules or substantial deviation from the "norm" will trigger an almost automatic audit by the I.R.S. An audit by the Internal Revenue Service is frustrating, anxiety-producing, and expensive in terms of time of preparation, possible court costs, and the inevitable disallowances. Rarely does an investor commit blatant fraud which could result in criminal proceedings, and *rarely* does the I.R.S. lose an audit. The I.R.S. wins approximately 90% of its tax audits—*i.e.*, the I.R.S. collects additional taxes (no matter how small) and the interest penalty on the delinquent taxes in nine out of every ten cases. It pays to exercise good judgment, employ good professional help in preparing or planning your taxes, and do not become enamored by the promises and fantasies of acquiring great wealth through "sheltered" income.

There are four principle types of depreciation that will be appropriate for almost all income-property situations. A general rule to keep in mind is that once a particular method is chosen, the method cannot be changed during your ownership of the investment property. Individual circumstances which are relevant to each separate investment property and each separate investor will tend to determine which method of depreciation is best. The four methods of depreciation are as follows:

1. Straight-Line
2. Declining-Balance
3. Component
4. Sum-of-the-Year's Digits

1. Straight-Line Depreciation

Straight-line depreciation is by far the most common method of calculating the annual economic decline of an income-producing property. The attractiveness of this method lies in its simplicity, popularity, and essentially conservative appearance. It is the method most strongly recommended by this writer except in situations where one of the other methods is clearly recommended by a professional tax consultant. With all methods except component depreciation, it is first necessary to formally sort out the depreciable items from the non-depreciable items, namely land (which "never wears out"), and establish the economic "years of life," or the estimated number of years of economic value remaining in the investment. Example: an eight-year-old tri-plex was sold for $72,000. The value of the land was conservatively set at $12,000. The remaining balance of $60,000 included the building and the personal property. The remaining economic life of this wood frame building was set at 20 years. This coincided with the mortgage and would likely withstand a test of reasonableness (I.R.S. insists that first-owner, new, residential buildings be assigned a minimum of 40 years' life). The personal property (wall-to-wall carpeting, drapes, appliances, and other non-fixtures obviously have less than 20 years of "real" life, and were assigned 5 years of life and a value of $1,500 per unit. The depreciation at the end of one full tax year was $1/20$ of $55,500 ($60,000 − $4,500 personal property =

$55,500), or $2,775, and the personal property was figured at $1/5$ of $4,500, or $900. The total depreciation for the first full tax year was $3,675 ($2,775 + $900). This "credit on paper" is deducted from the year's net income for the tri-plex before taxable income is computed. If, for example, the net annual income of the tri-plex was zero, all of the $3,675 could be deducted from the investor's total taxable income from all other sources. In other words, $3,675 of total earned income would not be taxed (hence, it is permanently "sheltered"). In the 20% tax bracket, this would be a savings of $735. In the 40% tax bracket, this would be a savings of $1,470! The following year the same procedure is applied to the original figures ($55,000 minus $2,775 and $4,500 minus $900) without regard for the investor's original equity, or appreciation gain in the property. The biggest advantages of straight-line depreciation occur in the first two or three years. After just a few years the investor will have an excess of equity dollars (due to appreciation, principle payments, increased rents, upgrading, etc.) relative to the standard amount of depreciation that can be taken each year. One solution to this apparent contradiction is to creatively turn the investment property over at a reasonably early time. Earlier turnover (creative sale or exchange) also reduces the problem with "depreciation recapture." That is, upon selling an investment property, taxes are computed by subtracting the following from the sale price: the original purchase price, cost of selling, *and* all depreciation which has previously been claimed! Hence, it is the I.R.S. that "recaptures" the depreciation. The capital gains tax (now 40/60) can appear to be staggering in situations in which there has been extensive appreciation and extensive depreciation to be accounted for. Also, the rate of growth during these "later" years of an investment is inevitably slower, perhaps much slower, than in the first two or three years.

2. Declining-Balance Depreciation

The primary distinction between straight-line and declining-balance depreciation is that the straight-line method takes 100%

TOTAL YIELD

The concept of "total yield" is necessary to define to understand the total benefits and the total return on original investment that derives from income-producing properties. The annual return on investment is not sufficient to account for the substantial profits that can result at the time of sale. Even these profits can be at times difficult to assess because portions of the total profits will likely be spread out over additional years as a result of installment sales, exchanges, reinvestment of proceeds prior to tax payments, and the variability of the individual investor's tax bracket. A major point to be made here is that the individual investor controls many options that can favorably influence the outcome of the "total yield" from real estate. Total yield, therefore, is the sum total of all financial proceeds of an income-producing property from the act of making an original investment until all financial transactions are complete for that particular property. Total yield is the retrospective measure of how an original investment performed on an annual basis. The four principle elements of a total yield are:

1. Cumulative Cash Flow
2. Cumulative Principle Gain
3. Cumulative Equity Gain (appreciation minus cost of sale)
4. Cumulative Tax Savings (depreciation/shelter)

SAMPLE MEASUREMENT OF TOTAL YIELD

The Wildwood Apartments (four-plex) were purchased for $80,000 on contract with an original investment of $12,000, or 15% down. The balance of $68,000 was to be financed for 20 years at 9.0% annual interest. Monthly payments were to be less than $612 per month—17% of the monthly payment applied to the principle. The taxes were $1,800 per year. The income/expense summary was as follows:

WILDWOOD APARTMENTS (four-plex)

INCOME		
Gross annual income (275/mo.)		$13,200
DEBT SERVICE		
Interest payment (510/mo.)		6,120
Principle payment (102/mo.)		1,224
EXPENSES (annual)		
Electricity	180	
Insurance	240	
Maint. (5% gross)	660	
Management	300	
Miscellaneous	120	
Taxes	1,800	
Vacancy and collection loss	264	
Water, sewer, garbage	300	
		3,864
CASH FLOW ($13,200 − $11,208)		1,992

Assuming that the figures indicated above remained constant for exactly 24 months, at which time the Wildwood Apartments were again sold on contract for eight times the gross, or $105,600. The seller paid a brokerage fee of 5% ($5,280) and received $15,840 down and a balance of $89,760 at 9.5% interest (a wrap-around mortgage) on a 30-year contract and with a minimum monthly payment of $755.00 for principle and interest. The first year of sale was an installment sale with *less* than 30% paid down, including any principle payments received during the first year of sale (actually $15,840 + $7,520 = $23,360, or 22%). The balance was refinanced and paid off by the purchaser slightly more than one year later. The *total yield* on the original investment of $12,000 at the end of the 3-year transaction was 77% per year! Compare that result to *any* other form of investment. The final figures were as follows:

1. Cumulative cash flow (24 mos.) $ 3,984
2. Cumulative principle gain (36 mos.) 3,672
3. Cumulative equity gain (24 mos.)
   Capital gains tax on $23,360 at the 30%
   tax bracket = $11,680 × .30 = $3,504 tax
   $19,856 − $5,280 broker fee equals   14,576

   Cumulative equity (end of installment
   sale 12½ months later) as follows:
   $105,600 − $5,280 broker fee = $100,320
   $100,320 − $80,000 original price = $20,320
   $20,320 + $6,800 (deprec.) = $27,120 (basis)
   $27,120 − $23,360 = $3,760 additional profit
   Also, $755 − $612 for 12½ months = $1,788
   Capital gains on $3,760 + $1,788 = $5,548
   $5,548 × 50% × 30% (tax bracket) = $832 in taxes
   Balance   4,716

4. Cumulative tax savings resulted from two
   years of depreciation at $3,400 per year.
   $3,400 − $1,992 (cash flow) = $1,408 per year
   of sheltered income. $1,408 of sheltered
   income for two years at the 30 percent tax
   bracket is equal to an additional income of   845

TOTAL YIELD: $27,793   WILDWOOD APARTMENTS

INDIVIDUAL INVESTMENT GOALS

Investment goals for each person are essentially personal, subject to change and dependent upon perceived opportunities. Some diversification of investment goals can offer protection against the eccentricities of a rapidly changing economy as opposed to an "eggs in one basket" strategy. The investment programs which "feel" suitable and offer a reliably good return on your original investment (despite the presence or absence of high rates of inflation) are likely to be appropriate. The investor's age, tax bracket, private aspirations, and available resources may all have a bearing on potential investment planning. The relatively young person with very limited financial resources might be a likely candidate to assume higher degrees of risk in terms of virtual "over-financing" to acquire older, marginal properties which require extensive upgrading and careful management. Buying and selling with only the occasional services of a sales agent can often make such properties pay. The professional who is cringing over the progressively higher tax brackets but who doesn't want a "second" career may seek professional consultation and management in the real estate field without becoming directly involved himself, and, of course, he must be willing to accept a lower total return on investment. Partnerships may be legally formed to "pool" investment resources, abilities, and liabilities. The older person may have a substantial capital gain "problem" to resolve or defer until he or she is on a reduced retirement income. Large numbers of persons in the economy have made a full-time career of real estate investment as part of a brokerage firm, or in a non-affiliated way. The diversity of goals to be pursued through real estate investment can often be "tailored" to meet many individual needs and circumstances. In Canada and the United States, especially, the real estate investment field is not exclusively dominated by a few powerful individuals and organizations. Persons with some initiative and daring can get started in a personal real estate investment program with little more than lots of determination.

RISK FACTORS AND GENERAL ECONOMIC TRENDS

The amount of risk that an investor should knowingly assume is basically a subjective issue. The consistently successful investor is the one who analyzes situations thoroughly *in advance* to avoid and/or reduce the serious "surprises" that may occur after an investment plan is initiated. The investor who pays "too much" for an income property and who also discovers substantial deferred maintenance after the fact is flirting with excessive risk. Rental properties are not all sold at a profit. Some individuals just can't get the rent collected. In other situations, many physicians, dentists, and attorneys have found it necessary to come out of retirement or semi-retirement to meet the "out-of-pocket" expenses for poorly managed and poorly maintained investment properties. Few sellers or agents of sellers will caution a buyer about potential mistakes they may be making with respect to price, or the cost to make certain improvements, etc. There are far more variables involved in the transfer of real property than in almost any other product, and there is rarely a warranty on any of the component parts, except "ownership" itself. The quick walk-through inspection is about all the typical buyer is even expected to ask for. One of the basic goals of this book is to suggest ways of identifying or protecting yourself against most of the severe risks inherent in purchasing any real property.

Income-producing property is generally purchased "by the numbers." That is, the total income is related to the total expenses (with the new debt service in mind) to determine how adequately the property will support itself with reasonable management and maintenance. The secret to improving the quality of those judgments is to verify those figures through actual vendors and to be especially sensitive to the probable areas of deferred maintenance and distortions about how much the monthly rents can be raised.

The income-property investor who repeatedly applies the same formula for investment without being open to change will eventually find himself in real trouble. If something works, a person often sticks with it despite changes in its usefulness. Trying something new appears to be "riskier" than staying with something familiar. The investor who starts out with an undeveloped building lot or a single-family dwelling is inclined to spend years duplicating that original experience. Persons who have relied exclusively upon real estate agents tend to think it is "natural" to continue to do so. The thrifty, ultraconservative approach to investing in a period of rapid changes of monetary valuation is equivalent to settling for a substantially reduced return on that investment. Thoroughness and professionalism as an investor implies study in many areas, "doing your homework," caution at one time, boldness at another, and adaptability to changing economic circumstances. The economy in a particular region as well as the nation or groups of nations is always in a state of some degree of change. Catastrophic changes (wars, major disastors) are events that individuals can't do much about. Lesser changes can be anticipated and adjustments made to the new circumstances. Tax codes are always changing. Interest rates are always changing. Consumer preferences are always changing. Zoning, laws, demographic characteristics, neighborhoods, cities, and almost every aspect of human behavior are in some state of change. Accurate anticipation of the general direction of this immeasurable number of changes in the economy will significantly contribute to risk reduction. A strategy that is based upon the unchangeability of some economic feature, such as continuous inflation-appreciation, will eventually have a tragic fate.

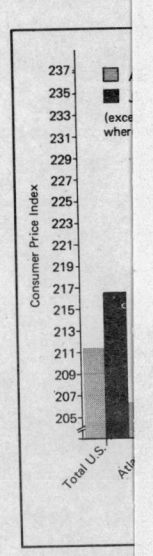

PRICES IF 10% INFLATIONARY TREND CONTINUES

	1978	1988	2008
Average Home	$60,000	$141,480	$885,665
Luxury Car	14,000	33,012	206,655
Economy Car	5,000	11,790	73,805
First Year College	4,000	9,432	59,044
Coffee (1 lb.)	3.50	8.25	51.65
Milk (1 gal.)	1.50	3.54	22.16
Cigarettes (1 pk.)	.60	1.42	8.89

INFLATION

Inflation is a topic which does not require as much introduction as it did a few years ago. At the time of this writing, the prime interest rate charged to favored corporate borrowers by the major commercial banks is *above* 15%! Oil prices have doubled and tripled since 1973. The increasing demand for imported oil by all of the world's industrial and pre-industrial nations will continue to drive the price even higher. Government expansion and deficit substantial discounts on their "list-price equities." Following the massive layoffs at Seattle's Boeing Aircraft Company in the early 1970s, there were large numbers of home-owners who completely abandoned their home equities if they could only find someone to come in and assume the existing mortgage. Most of those homes are currently valued at $60,000 to $100,000 and above. It's now difficult to believe that such a thing could happen again. Seattle was not unique. The Department of Housing and Urban Development is heir to a nightmarish number of abandoned and/or defaulted properties throughout the nation. Foreclosures and defaults on loans for residential properties, however, continue to be virtually unheard of relative to the rate of loan default and various types and chapters of bankruptcies that are taken out each year by small businesses, and a few that are not so small.

The liability that a low rate of liquidity presents is part of a complex interplay of the local economy, the financial strengths and needs of the property owner, and the perceived value or use possibilities of the property itself. It is typically the "innocent bystanders" who are hurt the most in short-term financial "panics." The investor who has made some provisions to wait out these brief downswings in the economy can avoid being hurt at all. Partial liquidity can be obtained by borrowing against real property at times when poorly secured loans are being denied. Liquidity can also be improved by setting a realistic and competitive current market price, not the idealistic price.

LEVERAGE

Financial leveraging has often been described as the use of "O.P.M.," *i.e.*, other people's money, to increase the return on an investment. The distinct advantage of real property investment is in the fact that it is tangible and virtually theft-proof, and therefore debt is almost always secured by the property itself in the form of a mortgage. It is a common occurrence to obtain 80% to 90% financing in the acquisition of income-producing property.

Not only do investors rarely have 50% or more to put down on an investment property; it can be demonstrated that it would be less profitable to do so!

COMPARISON OF $10,000 LOT WITH DOWN PAYMENT OF $500

A $10,000 lot was purchased with $500 down @ 8.5% interest and sold in 14 months for $12,000. The cost of possession follows: $9,500 balance at 8.5% interest for 14 months equals $942. The taxes were $200 per year. Taxes paid for 14 months equals $233. The total monthly payments of $1,175 are fully deductible and at the 40% tax bracket; this amounts to a tax savings of $470, and a net expense of $705.

The gross profit of $2,000 was subject to capital gains treatment—50%* of the $2,000 profit was taxed at the 40% tax bracket ($1,000 × .40 = $400), leaving a net profit of $1,600. The final result was as follows: gross profit ($1,600) minus the gross expense ($1,205) equals $395.

$$\frac{\text{Net profit of \$395}}{\text{Orig. invest. \$500}} = 79\% \text{ return on original investment!}$$

COMPARISON OF $10,000 LOT WITH DOWN PAYMENT OF $5,000

A $10,000 lot was purchased with $5,000 down @ 8.5% interest and sold in 14 months for $12,000. The cost of possession follows: $5,000 balance at 8.5% interest for 14 months equals $496. The taxes were $200 per year. Taxes paid for 14 months equals $233. The total monthly payments of $729 are fully deductible, and at the 40% tax bracket this amounts to a tax savings of $292 and a net expense of $437.

The gross profit of $2,000 was subject to capital gains treatment—50% of the $2,000 profit was taxed at the 40% tax bracket ($1,000 × .40 = $400), leaving a gross profit of $1,600. The final result was as follows: gross profit ($1,600) minus the gross expense ($437) equals $1,163.

$$\frac{\text{Net profit of \$1,163}}{\text{Orig. invest. \$5,000}} = 23\% \text{ return on original investment!}$$

---

*Now 40%.

26 Real Estate Investment

The differential between the amount necessary to control a loan and the loan itself is referred to as "leverage." It is the principle of leverage which permits the entry-level investor and the sophisticated investor to gain a possessory interest in an income-producing asset. Controlling large sums of money with a minimum investment is one of the major objectives of assuming the responsibilities and obligations of income property. A deposit of $5,000, for example, in a savings account can be reliably expected to produce approximately $250 in interest at the end of one year. After subtracting the tax on the interest and the evaporation effect of one year's inflation, there will be a distinct *negative* investment return. However, by utilizing the principle of leverage, a capital investment of $5,000 can control a loan approximately nine times its size, or $45,000. If a third investor were to take $5,000 and the $45,000 in borrowed money to purchase a modest duplex, the return on $5,000 could be as follows:

A $50,000 duplex was purchased with 10% down ($5,000 with 8.5% interest on the balance of $45,000 for 30 years. The monthly payment for taxes and interest (no principle payment) was $402 ($319 interest and $83 taxes). The gross annual income was $7,200 ($300/month per unit). The gross annual expenses were 14% of the gross income, or $1,008. The gross annual income after 12 months ($7,200) minus the total annual expenses ($5,832) left a positive cash flow of $1,368. The straight-line depreciation on $40,000 for 20 years' life was .05 × 40,000, or $2,000. The $2,000 of depreciation was substracted from the $1,368 cash flow to create a tax shelter of $634. At the 40% tax bracket, this resulted in a tax savings of $254. The pocketed cash flow of $1,368 and the tax savings of $254 resulted in a first-year gain of $1,622.

$$\frac{\text{Net profit of } \$1,622}{\text{Orig. invest. } \$5,000} = 32\% \text{ return on original investment.}$$

The bonus is that the duplex appreciated in value at a rate of from 10% to 15% for additional profits (before taxes) of $5,000 to $7,500. The $7,500 + $1,622 = a 180% return on the original investment!!!

Leverage is the primary ingredient in the "creation-of-wealth" formula. When carefully and conservatively applied, the concept of leverage has made it possible for enormous numbers of individuals to create fortunes in real estate. The danger lies in the fact that leverage works in two basic ways—it can make a sound investment better, and a shaky investment worse.

2

Single-Family Dwellings

For the cautious individual who has not yet made an initial investment in income-producing properties, the most basic and by far the most accessible starting place is the single-family dwelling (S.F.D.). The rationale for consideration of the single-family dwelling as the place to begin your real estate investment strategy is almost self-explanatory. The single-family dwelling is the most common, most diversified, most practical, and most easy to finance "medium" of the various types of income-producing properties. The single-family dwelling (rental house) is a miniature model of the total real estate investment field. The same basic principles, practices, advantages, and disadvantages can be realistically learned and applied to economically larger investments. The same rules of depreciation, for example, can be applied to the single-family dwelling as well as the mini-apartment complex and even much larger investments*

Experiences which you, as a private individual, may already possess in the acquisition, maintenance, and disposition of your own home, or that of family and friends, may be readily transferred to the income-producing single-family dwelling with minor modifications only. Your own skills in evaluating the unique value and desirability of a house as a place to live from the point

---

*See discussion of the four methods of depreciation in Chapter 1.

of view of a renter or a buyer is readily transferred as the kind of judgment required for success as a part-time or full-time real estate investor.

The availability of single-family dwellings in virtually every community throughout the nation represents an almost unlimited potential for acquiring the right investment property to suit your particular investment objectives. Cash flow (cash spendable), equity growth, financial independence, tax shelter, profits from sale, retirement nest egg, inflation hedge, wealth, financial security, change of career, and others are potential objectives which may be realized either partially or completely, and, with tenacity and good judgement, exceed your greatest expectations! Every residential community possesses older homes in varying states of neglect or decline which have the potential to become profitable income-producing properties. A good supplementary reference on this subject can be found in Albert J. Lowry's *How You Can Become Financially Independent by Investing in Real Estate* (Simon and Schuster). He looks for dwellings that have what he calls a "valuable fault," *i.e.*, a conspicuous problem that will permit effective negotiation on the price but can be resolved at a reasonable cost. Common examples would be peeling paint, neglected landscaping, dark hallways, tacky entrances, antiquated appliances or fixtures, or perhaps an absent, incompetent, or negligent property owner. These are common situational problems that you can inexpensively correct. In attempting to remedy "big problems," it can quickly become apparent when such dwellings are unrealistically over-priced, or too far gone. The solution is to flatly reject such properties or insist upon an "unrealistically" low offer to buy the property "as is." Various structural faults such as settling problems, leaking roofs or basements, severe wood rot, undesirable location, illegal room sizes, or generally poor design may be very costly to remedy and won't add a dime to the additional rent that should be produced. Tenants legally expect housing which is livable and free from any health hazards (plumbing out of order, heating system problems, insecure locks on doors and windows, water leaking into the building, broken windows, electrical hazards, etc.). Failure to provide a quick and agreeable resolution of such problems can result in court appearances, formation of tough tenant organizations, or malicious damage to the property by the disgruntled tenant.

REVERSING URBAN BLIGHT

The cumulative investment return (see "total yield," Chapter 1) makes it possible for even the smallest investor to partially or extensively reclaim declining properties and provide a necessary dual service to the community at large by reversing the trend toward urban and rural blight. Instead, you could be assisting to provide livable, attractive housing to persons who are temporarily or permanently unable or unwilling to purchase housing of their own. Demand for suitable private dwellings grossly exceeds the availability of such property. As more and more persons are economically prohibited from acquiring a new or older dwelling as an owner-occupant, the demand for quality rental properties will increase. In most residential communities throughout the country, the "average" cost of a new single-family dwelling is conservatively priced between $60,000 to $80,000 and up! Persons who have not acquired substantial equities in older homes or from other investment sources simply cannot handle the sizable down payments, closing costs, and huge monthly installments which must include high interest rates (11% and up) and related high property taxes. To the staggering cost of the monthly mortgage payment, the new-home buyer must also be prepared to pay for assorted monthly utilities, insurance, and general property maintenance. The "American Dream" of owning a home is rapidly becoming an illusion.

A "CORNER" ON THE HOUSING MARKET

If single-family dwellings are such a "hot" investment and each year offer a total yield ranging from 35% to 50% (and more) on the original investment, why don't the banks, life insurance companies, large corporations, pension funds, brokerage houses, and wealthy individuals "corner" the market? The answer, in the opinion of this writer, is that the volume and diversity of the single-family dwelling market is too great and too widespread both geographically and timewise to "corner" the market. This last statement can be translated to mean that the most probable reasons that the S.F.D. market cannot be cornered are the cost and management factors. Single-family dwellings are typically not profitable to large professional property managers, real estate investment trusts (R.E.I.T.'s), realty companies, bank trust departments, and so on because S.F.D.'s require a maximum amount of active management at various times in the economic life of each individual unit. The multi-million-dollar investor, almost without exception, is heavily involved in "major" real estate investments: apartment complexes, shopping centers, commercial property, industrial property, recreational property, hotels and motels, undeveloped land tracts, agricultural property, and others. The investments are essentially consolidated, not spread throughout the community like fleas on a dog's back. A single example should be sufficient to clarify the point. An investor with the capital to control a 100-unit investment property will likely confine himself/herself to one or at least several large apartment complexes to successfully manage the properties. At the other extreme, if the same individual were to acquire 100 single-family dwellings in some large urban area, he/she would have 100 different geographic locations to be concerned about. Incomprehensible amounts of time would be involved in the search, inspections, appraisals, offers, terms, contracts, conditions, rent schedules, maintenance concerns, mortgage payments, showing the property, *ad infinitum*. Disproportionately large sums of capital would be encumbered in 100 residential lots (500,000 square feet, or more!), and not one dollar of the value allocated to land could be depreciated. Typical investment portfolios of the BIG's do not include many, if any, single-family dwellings, or smaller, scattered plexes. The S.F.D. market will remain open to the small-scale private investor or group of investors who are willing to accept the "inconvenience" of traveling to a few different parts of the community to look after their investments and accept the "inconvenience" of personally managing different properties at different times and on different terms from the investor who controls mammoth investments and is satisfied with a 30% to 45% total yield each year after paying the expenses of professional management.

The small investor (*e.g.*, possessing from $1,000 to $50,000 to freely invest on a long-term basis despite the inevitability of financial emergencies) must assume the responsibility for all aspects of acquiring, managing, and disposing of an investment. The small investor can do everything himself/herself, or selectively obtain the assistance of a wide range of potential support services—attorneys, builders, tax advisors, laborers, real estate appraisers, building inspectors, real estate brokers of your choice (not randomly selected "sales agents"), fire inspectors, landscapers, material suppliers, property managers, certified public accountants, insurance agents, and psychoanalysts. The day-to-day decisions which demand varying degrees of seriousness must be attended to by some responsible party. A broken water pipe may require immediate attention. A new roof may require attention sometime during the economic life of the investment, if at all. The solution to most of the maintenance "headaches" is in the upgrading of a particular property prior to its occupancy, and especially prior to a profitable resale.

ACQUIRING THE SINGLE-FAMILY DWELLING

Much of the success in acquiring a single-family dwelling and related investment property begins at the time of searching for the investment "vehicle" which will most likely meet your investment objectives. In this respect there are two important elements of timing which may make the difference between a profitable and enjoyable experience and a minimally profitable and perhaps thoroughly disagreeable investment experience.

The first item of consideration is the somewhat philosophical question regarding the direction in which the economy is moving, has moved, and will likely move up to some date in the near future. In other words, is the housing market in a state of boom or bust, seller's market, a buyer's market, or neither? Are most of the properties on the market excessively over-priced? Are economic factors forcing sudden changes on residential living patterns? Are we moving into another *severe* recession, such as 1973, 1966, 1962, 1957–58, 1953–54, 1948, and earlier? Is the demand for a specific type of rental property sufficient to weather "hard times"? Can you withstand a chronic negative cash flow in a stubborn and severe recession? The answer to such speculative and personal questions and perhaps many related questions will never be wholly satisfactory. Investors did survive in 1973. Recessions reflect substantial changes in patterns of consumption, but people don't stop living in houses and apartments. Most people will make sacrifices in entertainment, clothing, and even basic food before risking the loss of their present "shelter." Vacancy rates tend to increase slightly as more individuals "double up," or tend to move in with family until employment and incomes improve. Over-developed or economically inefficient units will tend to suffer. The conspicuously over-extended investor will tend to suffer. Most situations will remain stable, and with strong inflationary pressures, income-producing properties could be the only reliably profitable investment "vehicle" during the recessionary period. Single-family dwellings are especially stable during periods of economic decline. The rate of foreclosures on single-family dwellings, as reported by the Department of Housing and Urban Development, is consistently less than 1 in 400. This extremely low rate of foreclosure is completely unparalleled by the foreclosure and/or bankruptcy rate for all small businesses. The small entrepreneurial establishment has perhaps one chance in twenty of surviving beyond the first two years!

The second important element of timing is the actual time of year when a single-family dwelling can be most profitably acquired. Certainly there are exceptions to a rule about the "best time of the year" to acquire income-producing properties. The general rule for successful acquisition and/or disposition of income-producing properties is to buy during the "off season" and sell during the "desirable season." Late spring and summer can be the worst time of the year to look for, appraise, and purchase a property for investment purposes (this general rule might be applied in reverse in such states as Arizona and New Mexico, where summer could be the best season to make offers). It is at the "desirable" time of the year that every white elephant on the market (as well as more desirable properties) is disguised with blooming flowers, a "fresh coat of paint," and well-trimmed greenery. The warm, sunny days and long hours of daylight appeal to the emotions of the buyer. The urge is there to rush in and make some of the necessary improvements on the property while the days are long and it's pleasant to be outside. This "fair-weather investor" is now in competition with a maximum number of buyers who will be willing to pay top dollar to a most grateful seller—a seller, incidentally, who may be able to walk away from a poorly insulated, leaky, drafty house with drainage problems, dry rot, and a broken-down furnace. The slightly exaggerated point to be made is simply that, advice to the contrary, the best likely time to buy cannot be the same as the best likely time to sell. In this writer's opinion, the most favorable time to buy is the illogical time. Cold, windy, and preferably rainy days in late fall, winter, and early spring are the best. The nastier it is outside, the better. Then, if the subject property and the surrounding neighborhood look attractive without the leaves on the trees, blooming shrubs and flowers, and that "fresh coat of paint," it will look even better during the remainder of the year when the leaves do return, flowers bloom, and the warm summer days move you to make necessary cosmetic repairs.

A more basic consideration is that due to the tremendous diversity in the style, construction, and seller "ethics" involved with single-family dwellings, adverse weather conditions, especially *cold*, rainy days, will alert the novice as well as the more experienced buyer as to what the major defects of the dwelling may be. This information is extremely important in the basic decision about accepting or rejecting a particular piece of property as a potentially profitable, or potentially disastrous, investment. The imagined inconvenience of walking around in the mud, snow, or blistering heat is substantially offset by the information gained and the more effective bargaining position with the anxious seller and/or the formally dressed realtor. It's like adding money to your account to linger around hard-working old furnaces, poorly insulated walls, doorways, and windows, or to carefully examine leaky, stopped-up gutters and down-spouts and notice the way the surface water collects under the building. Carefully timed bits of drama are important aspects of the inspection and negotiation process.* Don't overdo it. Hesitations, penetrating questions, and not dwelling solely on the negative aspects of the land and building are skills that often lead to *real profits* (see Chapter 6, "Buying Income-Producing Property at the Best Price"). Don't neglect the seller's most likely emotional status. The seller is typically experiencing a combination of pride, anxiousness, and defensiveness. The seller wants to sell for reasons which are frequently complex and only partially revealed to the prospective buyer. The sincere seller is essentially involved in a race for time. Within the first five to ten minutes of emphasizing a property's positive aspects, the seller wants to create a positive illusion that will permit the potential buyer to rationalize the negative aspects of the property (which may or may not need to be altered).

Oftentimes the potential buyer must relate to a broker or "salesperson" who has a certain expertise and in addition knows only what the seller is willing to openly or confidentially reveal and what common sense cannot deny. Example: sagging floors, wavy ceilings or roof lines, worn, stained, or burned carpeting, broken tiles, cracked, poorly patched walls, broken or cracked windows (absence of storm windows and doors), missing shing-

---

*See Robert J. Ringer's *Winning Through Intimidation*, (Fawcett, New York, N.Y., 1979).

les, inadequate or illegal-sized rooms (especially true about "extra" bedrooms) are rarely mentioned but become more "visible" with experience in looking at properties. Much more can be said in favor of conducting your primary search during the cold, unlikely, "off-season." Few buyers experience the "joy" of foul-weather house-hunting. In contrast, there is something very seductive about the warm days of late spring and early summer (particularly in the northern and mountain states), which seems to drive energetic "young" home buyers temporarily insane. Caring little for their own time and labor, they see the inescapable maintenance needs only in terms of the probable cost of materials to put things in order themselves. Seldom do they notice that the antiquated heating system may be barely operable, inadequate, and poorly maintained. Instead, they are mentally picturing the improvement that will result with new paint and new landscaping. Cosmetic landscaping is easy. A lot of cleaning up, transplanted annuals and perenials, and you're in business. Inevitably, the days will grow shorter, energy fades, and costs increase. The neglected plumbing and heating systems must now be reconditioned by someone who knows what he is doing. Filters must be replaced, fuel jets and chimneys cleaned, blower replaced, and a full supply of fuel ordered (optional) since the long-gone previous owner was entitled to use up, remove, or be reimbursed for any fuel left at the time of sale. Increases in the cost of fuel and in the amount of consumption by that old dinosaur may be more than you anticipated. You may begin to analyze the reasons for high heating bills, and perhaps you eventually discover that the walls, doorways, and ceilings are poorly insulated (not apparent on a warm summer afternoon). There are no storm windows tucked away in the basement. In fact, the basement is excessively damp, if not seriously leaking, throughout the wet season. The cheap coat of paint someone applied to poorly prepared exteriors before selling the building is already beginning to peel and flake. The gutters and down-spouts which were barely noticeable at the time are badly corroded, rusted, and the drain tiles, if any, are completely clogged. The glass in the windows rattles from a lack of putty, or a lack of rubber stripping in the case of aluminum windows. In the back bedroom there is a small but steady leak in the ceiling, which tells you only that there is a leak "somewhere" in the roof. The owner, whom you gladly "cashed out," has solved all of his or her problems connected with the maintenance of that property and is now comfortably living in some pleasant but unknown new location. In buying and selling any product, the responsibility to know what one is doing rests almost entirely with the buyer. The Latin expression *caveat emptor* ("let the buyer beware") has more validity in real estate than in most other areas. Knowledgeable investors tend to reduce the frequency and magnitude of buyer-seller errors. Some degree of error is virtually unavoidable. Avoid the *big* errors and you will prosper.

SIMPLE CONVERSION—HIGH RETURN

The single-family dwelling which is reconditioned and converted to a rental property is a first-class way to initiate and build an investment program which may ultimately take you completely out of single-unit rental properties and into large apartment complexes which are well located, in top condition, passively managed, and highly profitable. Favorable circumstances could perhaps lead you into commercial, industrial, recreational, or other combinations of investments which may more ideally suit individual backgrounds and objectives. A local investor spent years acquiring single-family dwellings, upgrading them, and then renting them with no other apparent goals in mind. The problem that this investor created for himself was to attain a very unwieldy number of scattered units, and he acquired too much current market equity in most of the units. In effect, he had lost most of the value to be gained from allowable depreciation and had instead created a significant income tax problem for himself. Uncle Sam was taking a significantly bigger bite each year. Selling the properties which had been depreciated out would have been even worse! By this time the difference between the depreciated-out "basis" and the current market equity would create an unacceptably high capital gains tax. The solution to the apparent double bind came from a local investment broker who was able to successfully convert the current market equities of the entire "bundle" into a tax-deferred exchange. The individual who had previously been "losing" money was transferred into a very large and profitable apartment complex with the maximum allowable depreciation to partially offset his greatly increased income. It was not critical that the low "basis" moved with him. The differences were quite apparent and gave this ultra-conservative investor many additional options to creatively rearrange his estate for himself and any designated heirs. The ability to make all of this, and further investments possible was the acquisition of the first rental house, and the next, and the next. Obviously, there are many variations on this very basic formula for the creation of wealth. Each person who attempts it will have somewhat different experiences and perceptions of the process. Success in meeting most of your personal objectives cannot be guaranteed. Initial hard work and caution throughout the process have resulted in substantial success for virtually all persons with the desire and tenacity to do well in income-producing properties. The basic elements and experiences to be acquired in the process do produce wealth and will allow the humblest novice to be financially independent through good times and the inevitable difficult times.

MANAGEMENT

The potential investor who is considering the single-family dwelling for the first time must be willing to become actively involved in the management of such an enterprise. Rental properties demand a particular type of management which is not at all similar to the management of mutual funds, for instance, or common stocks, real estate trusts, bonds, commodities, mortgage paper, rare objects, or small entrepreneurial businesses. At one moment you may be actively involved in providing or obtaining

Single-Family Dwellings 39

necessary services to recondition a particular property for rental or sale. At another time you must see that an electrical problem is resolved, plumbing repaired, rent collected, property shown, and so on. The distinction is that property management of single-family dwellings will be intensely active for a short period of time (not always the time that you would like to be giving up), and then all will be quiet (or effectively deferred). Even while you sleep* some advantages such as depreciation can be calculated almost to the penny. Other incentives for S.F.D. investment are more difficult to define. Pride of ownership and a sense of accomplishment can't be measured on a net-worth sheet. Qualities such as appreciation and/or profits of sale are very tangible assets which can be accurately determined only at the conclusion of the investment. It is through this unique form of management and perhaps 10% good fortune that you will realize substantial gains on your original investment. Overall, if you are not obtaining a 35% (or greater) annual return on your original investment, you are doing something very wrong, or perhaps you should look into a low-risk, low-return investment which will not make any demands on your time or individual skills. A good rule of thumb is that you should be able to double your original investment every two to three years (a 35% to 50% annual return!) as determined at the conclusion of the investment. A moderately conservative investor in single-family dwellings should be able to convert an initial $10,000 investment to $20,000 within a period of two to three years and *still* have the benefits of minor tax shelter, and perhaps a small amount of cash spendable from the property. Starting with $1,000, an investor would only have to follow this process ten times to become a millionaire! One thousand dollars to the tenth power equals $1,000,000. The scale is as follows:

$1,000, $2,000, $4,000, $8,000 $16,000, $32,000, $64,000, $128,000, $256,000, $512,000, $1,024,000

---

*Compare: *How to Get Rich While You Sleep: Let Real Estate and Land Do Your Work,* by David J. Huskin and William E. Monsees, Cornerstone Library, N.Y., 1969, 1970.

You can start from your present position on this hypothetical scale and count the number of years (approximately) that it will take you to reach a personal goal such as $1,000,000. Economic uncertainties will obstruct your ability to set a precise date. Inflation, however, will artificially accelerate this process for you. The rate of financial acceleration will depend mostly on your particular management style. "Successful management" of income-producing property is the key to reliably and cautiously multiplying your current investment.

With the application of basic rules and principles that will be discussed in more detail in the remainder of this book, any persons who are willing to purchase, manage, and maintain a single-family dwelling for themselves can quietly convert those and related skills into an investment program that will compare favorably with *any* other form of investment. Experience can be acquired at low risk and in a very private manner. Eventually, with continued confidence which results from sustained experience mixed with failure and success, the novice investor will ultimately want to consider such things as consolidation or diversification of investments, maybe professional property management, or perhaps such luxuries as one or more full-time employees to create wealth for you through maintenance and repair. The basic single-family dwelling may be an end in itself for the ultra-cautious or family-based investor. Confining oneself to single-family dwellings can be highly satisfying as a supplement to some other career that you may be pursuing. Rarely is "conflict of interest" an issue in combining the two fields. By itself, investments in single-family dwellings can provide the allure of self-employment, personal time management, and a much better than average return on your time and initial investment. The single-family dwelling investor assumes complete responsibility for all final decisions regarding almost all facets of the investment from beginning to end. Exceptions to this last statement might include conforming to local landlord-tenant laws, zoning regulations, property tax valuations, and subtle changes in economic conditions, such as a stubborn recessionary period. Personal decisions such as upgrading the quality of the present investment can be made primarily at your own discretion and can be proportionate to your current finances. Later, at least twelve months later, you will likely start making new personal decisions about the economic limits on upgrading, and shift to thoughts of refinancing, holding, exchanging, and a variety of "management"-related concerns. Real estate management at the entry level is typically a very "private" concern of the investor, the investor's family, and very few other persons. There is virtually no one around to decide when to push you into the next level of investment. After completing a particular real estate investment course and prior to acquiring the first apartment complex, this writer asked the broker-instructor if there would be an "advanced" course to gain a little more information (actually a little more confidence) about making such a move. The instructor's answer was, "This was *it!* You'll have to get your experience *out there*." Surprisingly, many aspects of the first "big investment" were a good deal easier to handle than most of the small-scale, single-family dwellings had been.

Active management is recommended .in the early and exploratory phases of real estate investment. In exchange for limited cash (or other convertible assets), the novice investor must assume a very active role in the management and maintenance of the first few single-family dwellings that are acquired. In some situations the novice investor, especially the individual or couple who are salary "rich" and asset "poor," must directly manage a tight-budget situation with a negative cash flow. That is, based on an analysis of basic economic conditions and. the strength of their current earning power, it can be a prudent decision to accept a financial agreement in which the anticipated income from a property is known to be less than the annual debt service and probably expenses throughout the year. This arrangement is commonly referred to as a "small alligator" because of the potential to be "eaten up" in the event of prolonged and serious negative contingencies that could impair the investor's ability to keep "digging deeper" for the necessary funds. The advantages, of course, are in the acquisition of an investment vehicle that could not otherwise be obtained, excellent equity growth in an inflationary economy, and above-average tax shelter. As capital assets progressively increase, more conservative and passive styles of management will become possible. Variable amounts of risk can be simultaneously assumed as the volume and complexity of your investments increase. In starting out with very little, be prepared to commit much of your own time and energies to the project. Consider, for example, the common fact that banks, real estate offices, and even professional property management companies are rarely (if ever) interested in directly managing a single-family dwelling. The reasons are pretty obvious. The potential benefits to be gained from a single unit usually will not justify having a "complete management structure" to perform the necessary duties, except as an emergency. If all of the management services were delegated at a cost of 10% to 20% of the gross annual income, there would be little if any immediate profit to be gained. The only exceptions might be the anticipation of a very favorable proceed of sale at some time in the near future and/or a maximum amount of tax shelter to be used by a person who would otherwise be in an uncomfortably high tax bracket.

Like the typical first-home owner, most entry-level investors who acquire single-family dwellings provide most of the management and maintenance themselves. They clean and otherwise prepare the dwelling to be rented. They advertise the availability of the rental through one or more means, show the property, collect rental (credit) applications, select the tenant, complete rental agreements, collect the deposits and the agreed-upon rental, oversee maintenance needs, indirectly supervise the property, and, in one way or another, terminate the rental agreement and start the process over again until preparations are made to convert the dwelling to cash, a "contract," or some other investment property (exchange). As the new "landlord" or "landlady,"* you will also assume some additional respon-

---

*Both "titles" are unfortunate terms which typically carry negative connotations and imply vague suggestions of possible feudal origins.

sibilities for very basic accounting and simple record-keeping, as well as a slightly unpredictable contingency of management activities during the life of each investment. For example, suppose there is a complaint that a neighbor's child was bitten by your tenant's dog and you were not even aware of the dog being there. What are the rights of each party in this or many other lessee-lessor situations? Usually day-to-day events involving rented single-family dwellings are rare, uncomplicated, and individually managed without incident. Learning to avoid some of the more complicated entanglements can be done through good judgment, careful attention to reference material, and a friendly relationship with your *own* attorney, C.P.A., broker, and insurance agent. The necessary learning you will acquire with the first few units will almost never be financially disastrous, and your carefully applied experience and economic guidelines will be immensely helpful as you expand the size and complexity of future investments. The high and increasing cost of just about everything almost dictates that the entry-level investors with less than ten units (allow some variation for individual circumstances and individual differences) will probably perform all of the management and most of the maintenance functions themselves. The reason is that the money and the availability of financing will not generally allow for professional property management or the extensive use of hired labor, private contractors, or union shops.

MAINTENANCE

The initial and ongoing maintenance of a rental house could be a prohibitively expensive venture if the investor had to rely upon skilled workers (private contractors and/or union shops) for each and every job. Especially in states where trade unions are prominent, the cost of doing those things which you would not attempt yourself should be carefully figured into the purchase price. The journeyman scale, which is generally doubled and tripled to allow for "shop" overhead expenses, can quickly mean disaster if major electrical, plumbing, or general construction work must be done.

To avoid some of the really large and unexpected mistakes in these high-expense categories, you must work out a discriminating buyer's strategy that will work for you. One such strategy is to make a personal inspection of the high-expense categories, and then at the time the earnest money agreement is being made up, you personally see to it that your offer *is subject to* an electrical, or plumbing, or other (specify) inspection and approval under the existing building code, and at the buyer's expense (this could be some of the cheapest dollars you ever spend, especially if the conclusion is negative and you can now exercise your option to renegotiate the price or abandon the offer without further obligations or loss of any earnest monies). For the investor, buying is much harder and requires much more sophistication than selling. Electric, plumbing, and structural problems will often be very expensive to correct when they develop into "major" problems. Also, these same problems usually cannot be deferred indefinitely and would most likely influence any attempt to resale. The investor must always be extra careful in entering into a purchase agreement that you establish some controls to minimize disastrous liabilities (*e.g.*, replacing partial foundations or supporting timbers, converting a cesspool or septic tank to a sewer connection, etc.) *before* you make the commitment to buy, not after. Some maintenance and upgrading is inevitable and should be anticipated with an optimistic attitude. In situations where you must call in skilled persons, you can often contact union members directly without calling the significantly higher-priced union "shop." You can legally do this by assessing what needs to be done and by contacting the union hall directly to request that one or more persons be sent out for an estimated number of hours and at the current journeyman's (or even apprentice) scale. The union business agents are delighted to get some of their experienced members off the waiting list, even temporarily, to prevent them from waiting around on unemployment compensation or perhaps drifting off to other communities. The cost will be 50% to 66% less than the hourly rate charged by the union contractor who is operating a business in the community with the inevitable high-overhead expenses. The primary distinction is that the union contractor "employs" journeymen (also apprentices and others) and provides them with a shop, materials, tools, advertising, accounting services, work orders, and fringe benefits, and must therefore pass on all of these costs to the consumer. As a consequence, the union contractors usually bid for and obtain large new construction and remodeling contracts at commercial job sites, and usually they don't want or can't afford to provide occasional quality services for the investor who calls in about some single-family dwelling problem once or twice a year.

Cleaning, painting, and landscaping contractors generally have lower or more competitive rates because they tend to be less technical, have less overhead, less union strength, and are more in competition with private individuals who "could" or would do certain jobs for themselves if the price were not at least reasonable. Carpet-cleaning is a good example. Small, private operators with quality, commercial-grade equipment installed in a van or small truck can often make very competitive bids to come in and thoroughly clean rental-unit carpets. The process and the equipment they use is far superior to the junky equipment that can be rented from tool-rental companies, or grocery stores. The carpet is much less likely to be saturated with potentially harmful water when done by the private contractor, and the rental lifespan of the carpet is more likely increased. In situations where you are perhaps less familiar with the work to be done and the cost of doing it, it can be in your best interest to obtain at least three competitive bids on each and every major job which must be done. Few contractors will insist upon a fee for preparing a bid. It is common practice for private contractors to be in competition with each other. Ideally, their different interpretations of the same problem will assist you in becoming more familiar with the actual details and costs involved. Selecting the private contractor you want allows you to make a management decision based on several different opinions and allows you to think over the situation rather than make a rash "yes" or "no" decision with the first contractor to come along. Admittedly, it is a good deal more trouble to obtain three separate estimates for the painting, three estimates for the carpentry, three estimates for the roofing, etc., but you are maintaining maximum control of the property management, and you will ultimately accept the bid (in writing, when possible) which promises to be the most economically feasible. This may mean accepting an intermediate-range bid rather than the lowest. Experience with both good and not-so-good private contractors in your particular area will become an important resource in helping you to estimate the real cost of upgrading and repairs for subsequent property acquisitions.

3

Multiple-Family Dwellings

Apartment units ranging in size from a minimum of two (duplex or two-plex) to a maximum of approximately nine units (nine-plex) can be acquired, maintained, and managed in much the same fashion as the single-family rental. The primary considerations in the selection of the two-plex on up to the nine-plex will be location, the general characteristics of the neighborhood, and the economic trend of that neighborhood. Small numbers of units such as these will ordinarily lack many of the amenities to be found in either single-family dwellings (privacy, extra space) *or* large apartment complexes. Typically, small numbers of units will lack air conditioning (except perhaps in the "sun belt"), recreation facilities, swimming pools, saunas, handball or tennis courts, 24-hour supervision, security, covered parking, FM-TV connections, panoramic views, professional landscaping, or interior design which may be offered by the extra-large complexes as devices to maintain maximum occupancy. Therefore, to remain competitive in good times and bad in this "in-between range," it is especially important that the property is well located. It should be very close to public transportation. The small complex should be near shopping centers and at least one good grocery market. It will also be helpful to be near other "public amenities" such as restaurants, parks, recreational facilities, churches, fast-food franchises, and "major" shopping areas. The existence or absence of these various amenities and others will have a distinct influence on the probable age range and interest background of the persons who will be your likely tenants. One good "rule of thumb" is to avoid a neighborhood where "everyone" works for the same employer. A recession in that company could have disastrous consequences for the owner of a closely funded six-plex, for instance, in which five of the six units are occupied by laid-off employees of that economically distressed company. Another good rule with the ownership of a small number of apartments is to give special attention to the comparable rents and comparable values of similar and related properties in the surrounding neighborhood. Make your selection as if you were going to refinance, sell, or exchange the property within a very few years from the date of acquisition. The advance and ongoing effort spent in researching similar properties in similar neighborhoods will assist you greatly in being able to act when you find a property that you *know* is well located and *not* competitively overpriced. In addition to posing as an astute tenant in search of an apartment, you can do a substantial amount of private research of different properties *before* you make a commitment to purchase a particular group of apartments. These recommended techniques for conducting a private market search before you make foolish commitments to purchase something on the market are discussed in some detail in Chapters 5 and 6.

The distinctions between income-producing properties that are single-family dwellings and those that are multiple-family dwellings are essentially a matter of quantity and quality rather than of kind. The Internal Revenue Service, for one, makes no formal distinctions between the two classes of residential investments. The skills, knowledge, and assorted problems that are common in acquiring and managing a single-rental unit will be common in acquiring and managing multiple-rental units. Initially, the increase in the number of units from perhaps a couple of rental houses to one six-plex or eight-plex *will* increase your responsibilities and obligations with respect to financing, tenant concerns (more rent to be collected, more turnover, etc.), increased maintenance, and increased needs for management. Sound too difficult? Wait! You can now afford some additional help. First, the I.R.S. is going to allow more depreciation because a substantially larger proportion of the purchase price can be allocated to the building and personal property, not land. For a small discount in the rent, you can obtain a resident manager who can be a "building-sitter," or perhaps much more, depending on the mutually agreeable terms. The consolidation of units on one site can mean less travel to monitor the investment, less landscaping, and a smaller percentage of the total investment monies going into non-depreciable land. At least by the end of the first 90 days of ownership, there should be a positive cash flow that will be adequate for most contingencies. Professional management and supervision of the resident manager by someone else can be obtained, if desired, for approximately 5% of the gross annual income. This last option becomes more of a reality as the total number of rentals gets to be above roughly 20 to 30 units. A resident manager's monthly rental discount and/or salary should average approximately 2.5% to 6% of the net monthly income. As the number of units and the net monthly income increase, so do the income and responsibilities of the resident manager.

SIMILARITIES BETWEEN SINGLE- AND MULTIPLE-FAMILY RENTAL UNITS

1. Financing and the use of leverage
2. Depreciation and the advantages of tax shelter
3. Similar operating expenses and cash flow
4. Flexibility in adjusting rent schedule (& gross annual income)
5. Tenant selection, vacancies, and collection losses
6. Leases, tenant rights, obligations, and laws
7. Provision of safe, clean, and healthy living environments with appropriately functioning utilities and basic amenities.

DISTINCTIONS BETWEEN SINGLE- AND MULTIPLE-FAMILY RENTAL UNITS

1. Reduction in square footage of living and storage space
2. Reduction in the amount of land per unit; less yard work
3. Reduction in privacy (visual and auditory)
4. More restrictions on parking, land, and building uses
5. Different policies regarding pets, children, and behavior
6. On-site management and reliance on others for maintenance
7. Expanded potential for income, appreciation, and tax shelter

As a result of the continuing pressures of inflation, the demand for single- and multiple-rental units will continue to be *very* strong until approximately 1984–87, when most of the baby-boom population (currently ages 21 to 35) settles into private residential ownership, condominiums, and cooperatives. The speed with which new apartment units can be constructed will result in the market being mostly over-saturated with "surprisingly high" vacancies for a period of years. The exceptions will be areas of rapid population growth, well-located properties, and properties which attract the over-55 age group and the middle- and upper-middle-income groups. The young people who are just "starting out" will become a rarity in the rental market, as they are presently experiencing among the school systems and colleges. These moderately predictable changes in migration patterns and the aging process within the population will result in a distinct over-production of rental units available in some areas and drastic declines in the occupancy rates which are currently steady at or near the 100% level.

The peak of the demand for rental housing is in the age groupings from 19 to 30 years of age, and over 55 years. The two groups are not mutually exclusive, but life-styles and interests seem to make it so. Whether intentional or not, apartment managers and the renters themselves usually cater to one age group or the other. The older tenants (over 55 years), who will continue to represent a large portion of the total population, tend to come from two different backgrounds—persons who are giving up a private home (widows, widowers, divorcées, incapacitated, retirees, etc.), and those persons who basically never could afford a home of their own (many will be on S.S.I., S.S.D.I., disability pensions, or merely have a long-term history of low-average earnings). The common needs of the older tenant will emphasize convenience and economy. Convenience to public transportation, shopping, churches, hospitals and/or clinics, restaurants, and other public facilities such as libraries, parks, museums, and civic theaters will be especially important. Comfortable units that are economical to heat and clean and mostly free from architectual obstructions (numerous steps, hills or slopes, long distances from one point to another, or inferior visitor parking facilities) will be essential with most older tenants. A strong need for security along with qualitative police and fire protection will be emphasized more by the older tenant. In contrast, the young tenants are likely involved in vocational preparation or early career development and typically have difficulty in obtaining the down payment and monthly payments for a place of their own. Inflation has made it progressively more difficult for the person or persons starting out to acquire and hold on to an acceptable property of their own. The majority of young renters are probably not even considering private ownership of property until a substantially later date in their lives, if at all. Convenience for the younger renter could also include accessibility to public transportation, but is more likely to mean a convenient place to park. The distance to shopping areas, restaurants, recreational facilities, schools, employers, and general places of entertainment can be somewhat more flexible. To remain competitive among the younger tenants who are prone to move around much more frequently, there may have to be special attention given to amenities within the apartment complex, such as recreation rooms, saunas, swimming pool, or perhaps a tennis court. The younger tenants will generally not be as concerned about minor inconveniences of the apartment, overall utility costs, stairs (up two flights maximum), and longer distances to walk from an apartment to the laundry room, parking area, garbage area, etc. Fire and police protection will be low priorities unless there is some specific reason for concern. For protection against break-ins or assaults (especially sexual), tenants of all ages are tending to insist upon well-secured deadbolts and peephole lenses in the doors as *minimal* precautions. Failure to promptly meet "reasonable" tenant demands has resulted in many court-ordered compliance orders, new legislation favorable to tenants, and some tough laws throughout the country which much more specifically define landlord-tenant rights and obligations. The owner-investor who feels it is possible to ignore this new tenant awareness and body of new law ("consumer rights law") is subject to fines, legally withheld rent, vicious counter-attacks from hordes of legal-aid attorneys, tough tenant organizations, and more (see Chapter 8 on tenant selection).

LARGER COMPLEXES

Apartment complexes with units ranging from ten to literally hundreds of units differ from the small apartment complex in six basic ways:

1. Degree of financial encumbrance
2. Degree of management and maintenance
3. Possible joint ownership, trusts
4. Diversity of amenities
5. Closer association with support professionals
6. Quality of income and degree of tax shelter

DEGREE OF FINANCIAL ENCUMBRANCE

The sheer amount of cash (capital) necessary to obtain a controlling interest in a larger complex can be immense. The larger complex will typically not be the *first* acquisition of the income-producing property investor. It is conceivable that the necessary funds could be derived from any number of sources (inheritance, for example), but it is most likely that the necessary funds will be derived from a lesser, yet similar, investment. Bigger investments imply bigger risk-taking, and this can be literally true when broad experience at "safer" levels has not been obtained first. If you put all of that "inheritance" into that "small alligator," you may have great potential for creation of additional wealth through leveraging, but, in the mean time, how are you going to pay for the unexpected problems and contingencies that need attention on very short notice? Can the property show sufficient value beyond indebtedness to be refinanced with a second or third mortgage? Do outside funds exist? Can rents be raised? Can rents be collected without "collection losses"? The reader may recall the comments in Chapter 1 about leverage—namely, that leverage makes a good investment better and a poor one worse! The relatively inexperienced investor must strengthen and protect that "bigger" investment by having some reserve funds, reserve assets, and reliable sources for borrowing additional funds in the case of an emergency or prolonged negative cash flow. Large apartment complexes must be researched and purchased with more care than with smaller numbers of units. The professional assistance of your own established attorney and certified public accountant is indispensable. Be fully prepared to reject investment situations in which the "numbers" are deficient, promissory, or simply do not feel right. Be prepared to be frustrated by sellers who want virtual cash-outs for their 50% and better list-price equities. Financing at this level will typically be less of a problem than it was to obtain your first conventional loan, because it is the seller who must assume many of the responsibilities of the banker. Thoroughly study the techniques of buying income-producing property on contract and then set out to pyramid your current investment-property equities into financially larger and larger investments until you reach your personal objectives. The financially conservative approach is the recommended one. Buy strong (high percentage of down payment) to obtain the right properties that will most closely meet your personal objective. Against a financially solid property, it is often easier today to obtain a $200,000 loan than it was to obtain a $20,000 loan for a small rental house years ago. When it is not strictly prudent or possible to be financially conservative, you might allow yourself to become discreetly "over-financed" only when the investment is "irresistible" in terms of the property's ability to support itself.

DEGREE OF MANAGEMENT AND MAINTENANCE

Apartment complexes with 10 to 20 units or more should be manageable with little more than periodic supervision of a resident manager (preferably a reliable couple). In the absence of an existing resident manager (a real sign of trouble if absent for more than a very brief interval), a new resident manager can often be found among the existing tenants who have good, verifiable credit references, and a good history of making the monthly rent payments in a timely manner. The amount of training for a new resident manager will vary substantially with the expectations of the owner-investor, the cash flow situation of the property, and the current vacancy rate. Poorly trained and poorly supervised resident managers will "lose" most of the qualified prospective tenants that would otherwise result in full occupancy (see Chapter 8 on tenant selection). The remainder of their responsibilities tend to come under the heading of "building-sitters," and would include such activities as noise and complaint management, *minor* maintenance, general monitoring of problems, and perhaps rent collection. The resident managers would not receive a rent-free apartment until the gross or net income was large enough for such an offset. A common rule of thumb is to allow the resident manager an offset equivalent to 5% of the net monthly income. If the resident manager's apartment rented for $300 per month, the net income would have to be $6,000, or a minimum of twenty units paying $300 per month. Larger units will tend to offer an apartment plus additional salary, a resident manager and assistant resident manager, or resident manager who is supervised by a team of professional property managers (usually for an additional 5% of the gross income). Maintenance will generally be sub-contracted to self-employed contractors or other service vendors. Sufficiently large apartment complexes will negotiate contracts with local maintenance companies for various services, or mostly rely upon the professional property management companies to provide maintenance services.

POSSIBLE JOINT OWNERSHIP, TRUSTS

Joint Tenancy refers to co-ownership of real property in which the rights of ownership automatically pass to the survivor following the death of one of the co-owners (irregardless of the content of the will of the deceased party). *Tenancy in common* refers to a variation on the joint tenancy theme in which one or more of the co-owners in a joint tenancy can legally convey their interests to a third party, thus making the third-party tenants in common with the joint tenants and entitled to a determined percentage of the ownership rights. *Tenancy by the entirety* refers to the situation of joint ownership exclusively between husband and wife. This designation cannot be used by other parties even though they are related. This form of ownership differs from the joint tenancy in that it cannot be severed by one party alone. Other forms of joint ownership which are often formed by individuals to facilitate the financing of large-income property investments are full or general partnerships and limited partnerships (which share many of the benefits of the full partnership with respect to percent of gains and losses, but they have no say in the management of the investment and they are liable only to the extent of their investment in that partnership). Additional forms of ownership that can be tailored to meet specific investment situations would include condominiums, cooperatives, corporations, and various financial trusts. These legal entities can be structured for use that is either independent or in combination to create formal co-ownership of an investment property. The formalities and technicalities of these legal documents make it imperative that experienced and competent legal counsel be retained to prepare documents that will be honored by the effected co-owners, the courts, and the federal government, if challenged.

DIVERSITY OF AMENITIES

The liability of concentrating massive numbers of housing units and massive numbers of supposedly homogeneous individuals in a confined area is that the "people problems" that are associated with congestion can be severely magnified. To offset this inclination and to remain highly competitive in a transitional market, the very large apartment complexes must offer an array of amenities that will appeal to the psychological and recreational needs of the prospective and current tenants. It is not at all uncommon for apartment complexes of 50 or more units to creatively advertise the customary rental space and, in addition, seek to create interest by describing the park-like grounds and bicycle trails, heated swimming pool, tennis court, indoor handball court, view of the city, private balconies, covered parking, closed-circuit television monitors for security, trash compactors, and so on. The very large complexes will vary somewhat in what they publicly advertise for the benefit of the prospective tenant and adjust for changes in the season and shifts in group preferences at the moment. The reality is that most newly constructed apartment complexes throughout the nation are uncommonly similar in their basic components. It is the location, price, management, and external amenities which account for the real attractiveness and holding power of a typical large apartment complex. The amenities are there to maintain that competitive edge. The necessary funding to make these "non-essentials" available often comes from the combined reasources of various investors who want the satisfaction of a favorable and reliable return on their individual investments.

CLOSER ASSOCIATION WITH SUPPORT PROFESSIONALS

Problems are rarely as simple as they seem. The day-to-day business world of the investor has become and will continue to become increasingly complex. Civil lawsuits are a grossly inefficient, time-consuming, frustrating, and *expensive* means of rectifying errors, omissions, oversights, misunderstandings, misrepresentations, mistakes, and the like. Whether we like it or not, the country and the world in general has become increasingly litigious. Everyone is potentially suing everyone else! Lawsuits are invariably compounded by counter-claims, delays, and myriad technicalities that ultimately lead to exasperating settlements out in the "hallway." The successful and survival-oriented investor *must* develop effective working relationships with a number of key professional persons. The four to five most important support professionals in the approximate order of importance for the income property investor would be: (1) a certified public accountant who is knowledgeable in most aspects of real estate finance, financial planning, and interpretation of current Internal Revenue Service (and related) tax law; (2) a licensed and experienced attorney at law who possesses a substantial background and interest in applicable real estate law, contract law, landlord-tenant law, and related legal matters; (3) a licensed real estate broker who can be relied upon for direct assistance, advice, and comprehensive investment planning within your particular community, and can be a major factor in the profitable acquisition and disposition of much of your income property (not the random broker or sales agent who just happens along); (4) a licensed insurance broker who can effectively handle all of your comprehensive insurance needs, assist you in providing the minimum necessary insurance to fully protect your changing estate, keep up with the changing properties, and provide general recommendations and advice; and (5) an institutional banker could be the fifth most important support professional to cultivate, since this could be an important part of your information about financial trends among the major institutions, a financial reference, and a source of reliable loan approval in times when additional cash is necessary.

QUALITY OF INCOME AND DEGREE OF TAX SHELTER

One of the major incentives for pyramiding income-property investments every few years rather than holding a few small properties for a lifetime is that larger apartment (or commercial) complexes *are more efficient* to manage and maintain than a few scattered pieces of property which soon exhaust their effective depreciation and, with persistent inflation, soon become "income-generating problems" which will have adverse effects upon your annual income taxes. It is through "unlocking" those real and inflationary equities periodically through refinance, sale, or exchange in a "upward" direction that allows you to preserve a favorable balance between growth, income, and taxes. A couple of rental houses and a duplex in different parts of the city are basically inefficient in terms of management, land use, and general maintenance. After just a few years inflation will have driven up the rent and the value of the properties, but the depreciation remains as a fixed percentage of the original purchase costs (minus the land). Too many dollars (real and inflationary) will be tied up in those three, non-depreciable lots. It is more difficult to obtain maintenance materials, or obtain the materials in large quantities, because the three properties are completely different. Management has to be a very personal thing because there is no potential to create a resident-manager situation among the existing, scattered tenants. The conversion of those accumulated equities into an eight-plex or ten-plex will create an entirely new valuation for depreciation and a substantially increased monthly income to meet the overall greater expenses. The "positive cash flow" from the two rental houses and the duplex may be substantially diminished for a period of time, but the income tax "problem" will be completely alleviated and the rate of growth on the small apartment house will result in a much more substantial "total yield" than the continued holding of the original properties. Holding an income-producing property more than two to three years in the currently inflationary market results in significantly diminished returns (see Chapter 10 on creative sale and exchange).

CONDOMINIUMS

There has been a distinct trend in the past few years to convert apartment complexes of some substance and quality into condominiums. The technical aspects of the conversion from apartment complex to condominium are relatively simple. The owner, or authorized representative for the owner, merely prepares a required legal document which formally declares the creation of the condominium and obtains the necessary municipal authorizations and formal recording after submitting a condominium record plat which describes in detail what the common elements and the unit areas will be. The seller would then proceed to offer fee simple ownership of one or more single-dwelling units (everything from the internal walls inward) to a variety of private individuals through the creation of their own recorded deed (if paid in cash) or mortgage (if financed). Each buyer in the newly created condominium will be a tenant in common with respect to all of the mutually shared elements of the multiple-family dwelling, such as the land, external walls, foundation, roof, stairways, halls, common facilities, and other components which are not formally described as being part of the living unit. The new owner assumes mutual voting privileges which are based on a percentage of the value of the unit owned relative to the value of the total complex. The new owner also pays a percentage of the common estate costs in addition to any remaining mortgage payments. This new condominium buyer is completely free to legally transfer title at will. The incentive of the original owner who converted the property from an apartment complex (under traditional real estate law) to a condominium (under condominium law) is an obvious economic one—the individual apartment units which might have been sold for an average of $25,000 each as a conventional apartment can be sold individually as condominium units for an average of $50,000 to $60,000 each! The ratio remains the same, roughly for properties with a higher valuation. Qualitative apartments in the high-growth areas especially are rapidly becoming condominiums, or being built as such, to absorb the intense demand for property "ownership" among the persons who cannot or do not want to purchase a private, single-family residence.

COOPERATIVES

An apartment complex can be just as readily converted to a cooperative through successfully completing the appropriate articles of incorporation and bylaws of a cooperative corporation. Otherwise, the basic distinction between a condominium and a cooperative is that in the latter the purchaser does not acquire ownership of a particular unit, but instead receives a basically long-term and non-transferable lease on a particular unit and receives shares from the corporation which are in direct proportion to the unit's value within the total complex. Cooperative and condominium owners both deduct mortgage interest and real estate taxes from their federal income taxes. Equity growth tends to be relatively minimal in both instances. Neither is recommended as a true, desirable investment.

4

Land, Commercial, Industrial, and Recreational Properties

LAND

One of the most often-repeated remarks of Will Rogers was a comment to the effect that there is only so much land, and they aren't making any more of the stuff! The implied message that has been popular for so many years is that anything in which there is a fixed supply and an obvious demand will be a secure and increasing source of value. The notion of endlessly increasing value following the acquisition and possession of land is further reinforced by the gross exaggerations of daily media saturation and the personal observation of select individuals who bought land at one price and later sold it at a higher price. One of the realities that Will Roger's comment neglected to point out was the fact that much raw land has changed relatively little in value (especially when adjusted for inflation) from one year to the next. A more cautious observation for the property investor would be that "usable" land tends to be significantly overpriced and it may be years before any significant "profit" can again be realized on that particular unit of land.

From the perspective of an income-property investor, raw land is considered to be any improvable area which is suitable for the construction of at least one or more single-family dwellings or other significant "improvements." Oftentimes developable land will be thought of in terms of acreage or large and loosely defined tracts of land on the fringes of some populated area. There are obvious "surpluses" of land all around us which appear to be dormant, under-utilized, or passively held by the government. In reality, most of this visible land is not for the casual, individual investor. Government lands, for instance, are rarely put on the sales block in a particular area, and then only in overwhelmingly large tracts and subject to "public" auction. The financing and development of former range lands, farm plots, and surplus government land are risky and technical undertakings which are beyond the realm of the novice. Substantial political, economic, and physical engineering problems must be overcome. Experienced corporate staffs and complex partnership arrangements are needed to convert large tracts of developable land into marketable "sub-divisions." These smaller portions of what may have been a very complex and time-consuming development may later be offered to "investors" under a variety of attractive-sounding names. Advertising phrases, such as Whispering Pines, Wilderness Paradise, Christmas Tree Valley, Sunnyvale Meadows, Seaside Estates, Smoky Mountain Retreat, and endless other possible names suggest investment potential and "peace of mind" which are often completely out of proportion to the actual physical and economic realities. Irregardless of the euphemistic descriptions and official names, these "pre-development" areas may well be inhospitable sites which are only partially accessible, *grossly* under-developed, and likely to be economically unfeasible for the promised number of residential and recreational dwellings that were planned. A startling exception is Lake Havasu City, which was developed out of the Arizona desert by the massive financial resources of the McCulloch Corporation. The unsuccessful, unfinished, and overpriced developments have grossly outnumbered the local successes. Few of these promotions have been priced within a range to offer an attractive "total yield" for an investor relative to the inflated sale price and the high monthly expenses.

It can be reasonably assumed that professional speculators,

corporations, and distinctly wealthy individuals have already acquired most of the readily convertible land within a reasonable commuting distance from populated areas. The novice investor who comes along in search of a small area of land for potential speculation or minor development of one or perhaps a few units will be negotiating with other real estate speculators rather than inexperienced and possibly naïve sellers. To do well in such a highly competitive market, the "small investor" should seriously consider the assessment and acquisition techniques discussed in this text to creatively identify and make offers for feasible vacant land sites *before* that site is placed on the open market. Not all of the sellers are going to be "hardened pros." However, this type of real estate investment can be more appropriately labled "speculation," since the intent in buying the unimproved land is essentially to buy at one price and to sell—at some later date—for a higher price. Everything rides on the potential for increased value. The essential ingredients of income production and depreciation will be non-existent. In fact, the exact opposite condition will be the case. The vacant land "investment" will represent a distinct negative cash flow situation throughout the period of ownership. Circumstances could potentially change with the external income capability of the "landowner" or of the external economy which could result in a desperation sale, refinance, or substantial holding period to make a reasonable profit on the speculated land.

The seductive message of the expression, "There is only so much land," can be twisted to justify the purchase of almost any piece of land and at virtually any price. The irrational logic of paying too high a price for a piece of vacant land and at the "wrong time" is thought to be justified because such possible errors will correct themselves as the land increases in value with time. A portion of the motivation may be that it is considered to be an even bigger error to not be in the land market at all! All of these notions are readily preserved by the accepted concept of limited supply and the observable (albeit unreliable) increase in demand. The stampede to acquire desirable raw land has produced immense wealth for some, and has at least frustrated or taken wealth from others. Desirable undeveloped land is principally the domain of experienced speculators, large commercial interests, and select individuals with unusually large tax shelter needs. Each of these groups is attracted to undeveloped land because each also has a *limited* ability and/or desire to provide the maintenance and management that would be necessary with an income-producing property. The novice investor, on the other hand, will likely do well to ignore the "unlimited prospects" of desirable vacant land until some more expeditious time (economically) in the future. One of the rationales for this recommendation is that "today's price" for desirable raw land is almost certain to be well above current, competitive market values. The relative scarcity of desirable raw land* causes it to be so over-speculated and overpriced that it may take years of putting money in until a good profit can be taken. The long wait for a profitable return tends to be especially true when you must pay an average of 7% in commissions to buy a desirable piece of raw land and a similar commission upon the gross amount to sell. The investor-speculator who can offset a 12% to 15% buying and selling fee in a short time interval and still make an acceptable profit has made a real accomplishment. Inflation, of course, often makes it possible for such seemingly unlikely events to occur. The risks being assumed by the investor, however, are increasing as basic land use and formal zoning requirements are becoming more stringent because of effective lobbying groups. Environmental concerns, militant neighborhood organizations, subsidized legal-aid staffs, and other special-interest groups can effectively lobby state legislatures to restrict the potential for development of remaining, desirable raw land. The result can be a significant decline in the value of a piece of land that can no longer be developed in an approved and feasible manner. The

---

*Builders, developers, speculators and others continuously and systematically scour local residential and commercial areas for possible building sites. Realtors and sales agents are continuously searching and advertising for such property. Daily newspapers are filled with ads asking for land to buy.

other potential for "upgrading" the zoning statuses to a "higher and best use" may be extremely remote and expensive for one individual to accomplish. There may be undetected problems which seriously affect the resale value of a piece of raw land. Absence of year-round accessible roads, absence of feasible waste-disposal possibilities, problems in obtaining usable water (*e.g.*, seriously fluctuating water table), excavation problems, unstable soil and/or erosion, development restrictions, environmental restrictions, utility service problems, and related expenses or complications can be economically disastrous to resolve. The prudent investor in desirable raw land will research each of the potentially negative contingencies, obtain professional assistance as necessary, and secure some degree of contractual protection for those areas which cannot be formally and accurately assessed in advance. Otherwise, it is entirely possible that the optimistic investor who expects to passively upgrade the value of a particular piece of raw land in little more than one to two years may not experience such an optimistic result.

There are two distinct limitations associated with speculation in desirable raw land. The primary limitation is that there is *no income* produced by the land,* and the secondary limitation is that *no depreciation* can be claimed on the ownership of the land. Hence, in addition to the "modest" down payment and closing costs, the "lucky" buyer must dig up the monthly interest, tax payment, and optional principal payment from other sources. Under these circumstances, and to get a good sale price, it's not surprising that a buyer can often negotiate a very low down payment and perhaps a favorable interest rate with the seller. The advantage for the buyer is that the interest and property taxes paid each year will be totally deductible from the buyer's personal income taxes.** When taxable income is derived from

---

*Exceptions would be rare instances where the land may be leased for extended periods of time for commercial or agricultural purposes.

**The return or "recapture" would be a function of the amount paid and the investor's final adjusted tax bracket for that year. That is, in the 50% tax bracket the buyer could reclaim the equivalent of one half of the total interest and taxes paid on the land during that calendar year.

other sources, this deduction can make a distinct improvement upon the buyer's tax situation. For basic economic growth, the purchase of desirable vacant land at a reasonable fair-market price can be an excellent investment. The eventual total yield on the land purchase will substantially out-produce any taxable savings account. And, like a savings account, there is basically no maintenance, management, or unexpected contingencies to be concerned about in owning a vacant piece of land. A legally recorded contractual interest, equity interest, or titled interest in developable land is virtually impossible to lose, have stolen, or in some way destroyed. Further, if held long enough to assure a good equity position, raw land can be an excellent source of collateral in obtaining refinance monies or in arranging for a tax-deferred exchange.

For reliable economic growth, the acqusition of developable land will invariably out-produce the best certificate savings program. The potential for the desirable use of financial leverage is excellent. The "problem," however, remains that there is no one to assist in paying off the newly acquired indebtedness except yourself. Tax-wise, there will be little or no deductible expense other than the interest and property taxes, which must be taken out of your own pocket each month. In some cases the odd lot which is purchased in some obscure location and with little or no money down is apt to remain exactly the way it was. A loss may even have to be taken in the event of a prolonged recession (*e.g.*, loss of your own basic source of income), or when extra monies are unexpectedly and urgently needed, or if in some way it becomes progressively more difficult to make the monthly installment payments. The absence of depreciation (I.R.S. rule: "Land doesn't wear out") seriously diminishes the value of vacant land as a tax shelter. The vacant-land speculator essentially gambles on the ability to use a maximum amount of leverage to control a "promising" piece of vacant property until it can be profitably sold. Inflation alone will often lead to good paper profits within the first year or two. However, to "unlock" these profits it will be necessary to creatively market and sell the property (by yourself when profits are thin) and make the best possible use of the four main tools of the seller: (1) direct sale; (2) installment sale; (3) refinance; or (4) tax-deferred exchange. The most typical method of sale, of course, will again be the installment sale, in which the seller now assumes the role of the "banker" until the deadline of the final balloon payment, or the property is again resold.

COMMERCIAL PROPERTY

Small, qualitative commercial properties are typically not available to the entry-level investor. The entry cash requirement and the potential of a sustained vacancy until a suitable tenant can be found, accommodated, and signed up under a long-term lease will be beyond the means of most novice investors. These same qualities can be ideal for the investor who wants to decrease the amount of active involvement in management and maintenance of residential units and who does not want to rely entirely upon "professional property management." Commercial property* can be highly desirable from a number of different aspects. A sampling of the desirable advantages would include: (1) high tenant stability; (2) good tenant credit references; (3) long-term leases; (4) "open to the public" visibility; (5) low maintenance; and (6) excellent overall return on investment. A more detailed description of the advantages of commercial property compared to residential property would be as follows:

1. High Tenant Stability

After living with the apparent instability of the month-to-month residential lease, it can be a very welcome opportunity to sign a long-term lease with a commercial tenant. The credit-conscious new tenant will often be as interested in establishing an image of permanency as the owner is to reduce the management and maintenance concerns that are produced by high

---

*Retail and wholesale establishments, office space, garages, shops and service stations, smaller motels and hotels, restaurants, and related public-oriented properties.

residential tenant turnover. It can be reasonably anticipated that the commercial tenant (especially the tenant with desirable credit and rental references) will occupy the property for at least the defined length of the first lease and perhaps negotiate many trouble-free extensions. A property, in return, which facilitates the slow, stable growth of business for the commercial tenant; convenience of location and parking for the customers, will persevere when similar small businesses are going bankrupt. The physical and financial stability of the tenant in a small commercial property will allow the owner to devote more attention to other matters and yet preserve all of the benefits of income-property ownership and the eventual appreciation.

2. Good Tenant Credit References

The commercial tenant has a financial commitment to the property to be leased which is not typical of the residential lessee. A financial identification will tend to be made between the business-operating tenant and the property itself which is important to the success of that business. The commercial tenant generally works to build relationships with customers and community vendors to convey the idea that this new proprietorship will be around in the reasonable near future and will continue to offer the services and/or products that it is presently providing. For these reasons and more, it is critical to select commercial tenants with established and verifiable commercial rental histories whenever possible. In either case, it is imperative to consider only those persons with verifiable credit references. Special care must be taken to avoid the judgment-free or potentially bankrupt commercial tenant because of the extended collection loss problems that could develop. Care must be taken to avoid leasing a commercial property to a marginal individual due to the uneasiness of having a vacant property for more than the average length of time. It is much wiser in the long run to attract the tenant who will need substantial modifications before occupying the premises than to wait for the tenant who will require little or no modifications to suit his business purposes.

3. Long-Term Leases

The stability of the commercial tenant is basically assured by negotiating and signing a legally binding, long-term net lease. It is an almost universal business practice for commercial properties to be placed on long-term net leases. These formal financial agreements are often referred to as "net, net," or even "net, net, net leases" to convey the understanding that the tenant is to pay the agreed-upon rent per square foot each month *and* the formally prescribed utilities and related expenses. The term "net, net, net lease" implies that the tenant has agreed to pay all costs, including the actual mortgage payment, insurance, and taxes! Such leases will generally be negotiated and written to be effective for *at least* one year. Renegotiated leases are commonly signed for multiples of at least five years and include allowances for annual inflationary adjustments. The total cost of the lease is a deductible business expense for commercial tenants and allows them to acquire temporary "owners' rights" to a business property which they perhaps could not afford to acquire and successfully maintain. The lease agreement frees the commercial tenant from the obligation of putting up substantial down payment monies to acquire the right business property (assuming it's available) and the additional cost of possible major renovation or remodeling to satisfy specific business needs. Also, the commercial lessee is not so bound to that one fixed-size property and the obligation of formally disposing of the property before moving to another location.

4. "Open to the Public" Visibility

In contrast to the private residential dwelling, commercial property (whether wholesale or retail) is typically open to the public during conventional business hours. With the need to serve the public and to project an image of orderly, competent management, the commercial lessee is socially obligated to maintain the property in a safe, secure, clean, and socially acceptable condition. The commercial property with obvious deferred maintenance or cleaning deficits immediately projects an image of deficient business relationships, a "don't give a damn" attitude, and perhaps inferior products and service. The success-oriented commercial enterprise will therefore have an accountability to the public at large, as well as to themselves and the actual owner of the property. Under such circumstances, leased property will typically be exceptionally well kept and maintained or even improved upon without significant demands or costs being transferred to the property owner. The actual owner can in turn make periodic "inspections" of the interior and exterior of the commercial property without the usual formality of written notices or the mystique of waiting until the residential tenant completely vacates the premises before actually discovering the condition of the rental unit. The commercial property owner, in effect, has the basic equivalent of "professional property management" without the actual cost of such a service. The predominantly absent and/or unavailable commercial property owner (especially if a large number of units or square footage is involved) will likely want to contract for additional professional property management services, anyway.

5. Low Maintenance

The maintenance concerns of the commercial property owner will be dictated largely by the type of business and the special requirements of the tenant who will occupy the available space. Some preparatory maintenance and general upgrading may be done upon initial acquisition or prior to being advertised for a new tenant to orient the property toward a particular type of business and to upgrade that critical rental rate per square foot prior to the lease-negotiation phase. After agreeing to accept a particular type of commercial tenant, the owner or owner's representative will work out the details of the initial maintenance and/or modifications to be done. Upon the completion of the basic required remodeling of the property, it will be the responsibility of the tenant to provide basic maintenance services unless excluded in the lease. Items that might be excluded in the lease could be separate cleaning services, major repairs such as leaking roofs, electrical or plumbing repairs, or correction of a major structural, safety, or health problem. The tenant with the "net, net, net lease" may contractually agree to provide all necessary cleaning and maintenance and related services during the period of occupancy.

6. Excellent Overall Return on Investment

The economic similarities between residential rental units and commercial rental units is much greater than either would be to land that is held for investment purposes. Commercial property always produces an income. Ideally, such property will be more than fully supporting after deducting the costs of taxes, interest, insurance, maintenance, *and depreciation*. The potential exists to resourcefully adjust the maintenace costs, improvements, and other expenses relative to the total income received each year to create the desired positive or negative cash flow that will satisfy a portion of the commercial property investor's annual objectives. In addition to the generally trivial principal gain, the commercial property investor can generally anticipate favorable appreciation gains following a relatively short period of nearly maintenance- and management-free ownership of the property.

MOTELS

The "right" motel (approximately 6 to 20 units) can be one of the best real estate investments in terms of income production. The well-managed and well-maintained smaller motel or motor hotel combines the assets of an independently operated small business with the full advantages of a real estate investment. A privately run complex of 6 to perhaps 20 units can be comfortably managed by an owner-occupant or a *well-supervised* resident manager. The hours, of course, will be absurdly long at times, but the potential for a strong, positive cash flow can be well above the average for equivalent amounts of leased square footage. Extreme caution, however, has to be exercised in obtaining the "right" motel unit. The risks in owning and/or operating a smaller (non-franchise) motel complex can be substantial. Small motels are highly susceptible to the following adverse factors:

1. Changes in the major highways or in general traffic patterns
2. A lack of full visibility (from a distance) from the road
3. Changing consumer preferences along with drastic changes in spendable income per capita
4. Other competition, or genuine potential for competition, in the same general area

A sudden change in the interstate highway system or a major arterial can result in the prolonged or sometimes sudden death of the motel business. The motel which cannot accommodate large groups at the desired times must rely extensively on the transient businessperson, tourists, and the individuals who are temporarily in transit from one more permanent dwelling to another. Even subtle factors such as impaired visibility from the road (even at a distance) or impaired accessibility (steep inclines, stairs, or other unimproved architectural barriers) can have adverse effects upon the steady volume and constant turnover that are necessary to make a small motel unit financially successful. Perhaps the most difficult variable to anticipate and cope with is the occasional changes in consumer preferences. One of the consumer risks is to be caught going in the "wrong" direction when the majority of potential consumers are moving toward either economy units or luxury units. A careful survey of ongoing occupancy rates and basic financial conditions in the economy at large should alleviate much of this concern. Another criterion of stability with the consumer public would be a detailed study of the cash flow (week-to-week) for the past few years and the frequency of owner turnovers within the last three to five years. Possibly a number of optimistic owner-managers have failed to make a satisfactory return at that particular location. The property must be analyzed as a small business as much as it does as a real estate investment. Factors such as "market analysis" and analysis of real or potential competition in the vicinity are critical along with the extra-thorough property analysis and basic financial analysis.

There are some unique characteristics of smaller motel units that can be relatively difficult to assess. Motel owners who rely upon resident managers must establish discreet criteria to evaluate the manager's potential "dishonesty" and/or "laziness." The potential for creatively "stealing" from the absent motel owner is relatively easy. Also, the hired resident manager who wants to sleep through the night may turn on the "No Vacancy" sign before the last units are actually rented for the night and thereby ignore the potential to rent all of the units. This particular problem can be rather difficult to detect unless spot checks are made to compare the reported rental records and the appearance of the "No Vacancy" sign. Another symptom of "laziness" can be the apparent lack of hustle in preparing the available rooms early in the morning. This lack of an available room due to a lack of readiness can also result in prospective occupants being turned away. A lack of thoroughness in cleaning and inspecting the rooms each time is also a distinct indicator of trouble that will have a deleterious effect upon future occupancy rates. One of the most devastating things that can happen to a small motel complex is to have "overnighters" publicize the lack of cleanliness or lack of privacy (walls too thin and/or poorly insulated) in the local restaurants, etc., before they travel out of town. Travelers who could otherwise become regular occupants will quietly go elsewhere. The first mentioned problem of "dishonesty" among resident managers can also be a real problem among small motels. A number of things must be done to detect possible dishonesty and to *dismiss* individuals who are definitely involved in such practices. The owner must often simply take the manager's word for the number of units that were actually rented during each 24-hour interval. One of the suggested methods for detecting dishonesty is to keep a very careful count of disposable items such as plastic drinking glasses, courtesy bars of soap, and matches. Especially, keep an accurate count of the sheets and towels that are sent to local cleaners and perhaps the coins that may be put in each room's possible vending machines. The presence of consecutively numbered receipts are too easily circumvented by maintaining two sets of books and thereby skimming off the occasional cash rental payment.

The successful operation of a small, non-franchise motel is quite possible when there is constant attention to providing diligent and honest management day after day to establish a positive reputation and to build a "clientele" in addition to the impulsive or non-discriminating transient who may be a "one-nighter" only. Small motels do not have the budget for saturation advertising and other amenities which are offered by the franchise-type of motor hotels. The smaller motels do much more business through competitive pricing and word-of-mouth reputations than might be casually assumed. Assertive and friendly management is critical for this combination of small business and real estate investment. The location and visibility to heavy traffic patterns will be critical determinants of a motel's potential for above-average financial returns. To remain competitive the rooms must be spotlessly cleaned, basically sound-proofed; have secure locks and doors, trouble-free plumbing and hot-water supplies, individual phones, attractive furnishings with quality wall-to-wall carpeting, color televisions in each room, ample parking, absence of architectural barriers, and miscellaneous amenities which may be expected requirements for economic survival in your particular area.

INDUSTRIAL PROPERTY

Industrial property is considered to be mainly an area of substantial specialization and not an attractive area for the casual or inexperienced investor. The risks in acquiring industrial property can be considerable. The primary cause of the high degree of risk is that most industrial properties were designed to meet the specific needs of one particular business concern, and that facility likely will not be readily transferable to a different industrial tenant. External economic conditions and the availability of money have a very direct bearing on the feasibility of occupying a new industrial-lease site. Also, rapid changes in industrial technology, equipment requirements, and marketing priorities can adversely affect the industrial-property investor. Industrial property can be difficult to profitably lease year after year during periods of high inflationary rates. The reason for this discrepancy is that industrial properties have the slowest average rate of turnover of all possible real estate investments. The predictably slow turnover rate is due to a number of identifiable factors such as unique building designs for specific industrial purposes, the high cost of relocating in another specialized facility, the dependence upon local experienced employees, and the de-emphasis upon real estate as an investment in itself by the industrial user. The typical industrial user will actually show a virtual contempt for typing up working capital in a "passive" industrial real estate investment by considering a lease situation only, or of constructing an industrial property and then immediately selling the property to one or more investors on the condition that a binding, long-term "lease-back" contract can be acceptably negotiated. The industrial tenant can now claim depreciation on all equipment and deduct *all* of the annual lease expenses (land would have been a non-depreciable holding item, anyway) *and* typically earn a quicker, if not higher, return on the exempted working capital.

For the investor the capital requirements to control industrially zoned property with an attractive amount of square footage (building and land) will usually be quite substantial. Also, the competition with powerful special-interest groups in obtaining and retaining permission to establish and/or operate virtually any new industrial concern is a major time- and money-consuming activity that is not the bailiwick of the ordinary income-property investor. Established companies which are intent upon relocating in a new area could often devote more attention to and apply the basic techniques of real estate investment more to their advantage. Studies by the chamber of commerce have shown that industrial concerns tend to relocate on the average of only once every 20 years. The resistence to change once an industrial concern is established may appear to be natural, but such longevity tends to spoil an otherwise desirable real estate investment. The land and buildings that are being purchased by the industrial concern will become completely amortized and depreciated out (based on pre-inflationary values) during this long interval. Periodic refinancing will increase working capital and create a deducation for interest but will not otherwise improve the situation. Also, once the building and equipment are totally depreciated out, the capital gains taxes will be grossly prohibitive unless an appropriate tax-deferred exchange can be equitably arranged. The changes in the external economy and the surrounding population tend to be much more rapid than the slow-moving changes of the industrial concern. The industrial company may now be seriously encroached upon by other types of development, such as residential units, recreational areas, expansionistic new firms, escalating property taxes, changes in highway or transportation systems, and so on. The local property-tax base and the surrounding labor pool may have changed drastically. One solution for many of these changes has been the accelerating migration of entire companies from the industrialized Northeastern states to the South, Southwestern, and Northwestern parts of the United States. In addition to perhaps establishing a new real estate "basis," the rationale for such a preponderance of moves can be summed up in terms of lower property taxes, lower corporate taxes, greater availability of less expensive land, lower year-round energy costs for heating, desirable labor pools, and the economic desirability of modernization of entire companies. The consumer market itself is decidedly moving in the same general direction and away from the Northeast and Midwestern parts of the country.

RECREATIONAL PROPERTY

For many of us it is most tempting to ruminate about the possibilities of acquiring a second home—a "cabin" in the mountains, a beach home, a fishing (or hunting) lodge, a permanent campsite, and so on—which would combine pleasure and profit. The colorful advertising which promises "peace and quiet," beautiful sunsets (or horizons), "recreation for the whole family," freedom to get away from it all, and related descriptive phrases may work on your imagination and become something in your mind that in reality is much different. The dissatisfaction that is commonly experienced with isolated "retreats" often comes from these distorted expectations. The burden of keeping up those "other mortgage" payments can, like vacant-land investments, be most trying when other demands begin to take precedence. The Internal Revenue Service will very carefully scrutinize any claims regarding income from a second residence. The 1979 edition of *Your Federal Income Tax, Publication 17* outlines the formula for allocating between personal use and rental use of a recreational property: "If you own and rent out a vacation home or other dwelling unit that you also use for personal purposes or as your principal residence (even for one day during the tax year), you must allocate your expenses.

"*Exception:* If you use the unit as a residence and it is rented for less than 15 days during the year, no deduction for rental expenses is allowed. However, if you itemize your deductions on Schedule A, you may deduct your interest, taxes, and casualty losses. Any rent received is not included in your gross income."[*]

Recreational properties have their best frequency of sale and price of sale during obvious economic boom periods and periods of rampant inflationary spirals. The exact opposite is true during severe recessionary periods and periods of economic uncertainty. Retirement communities, for instance, are often located in reasonably to highly desirable recreational areas. It's only natural that retired citizens will be more enticed by broad recreational opportunities rather than by stark, economical housing units only. The current popularity of all forms of recreational property has resulted in much over-construction in different parts of the country. For this reason alone it is especially important to utilize the appraisal and negotiation methods that are described in the

---

[*] See *Your Federal Income Tax, Publication 17*, 1979 edition, Chapter 11, page 42.

next three chapters* before considering the purchase of recreational property. The potential for doubling your investment every two to three years will traditionally not apply to recreational properties. The reason for this low average return with recreational properties is that building site costs are proportionately much higher than would be the case with typical urban or rural residential property sites. The risks assumed by the builders are therefore greater (plus commuter distances to worry about); therefore acquisition prices will be high. Investors and/or speculators will be in direct competition with concurrently employed couples who are able to financially and emotionally indulge themselves. These high-spendable-income (and tax-ridden) couples may not be so concerned about such questions as the ratio of value to indebtedness, cash flow, depreciation, and so on. Such instinctual and emotionally oriented buyers tend to be highly capricious and economically unreliable. An energy crisis, for instance, can have a profound effect upon the sales and values of recreational properties which are remote from large population areas. Lenders will become ultra-cautious about approving recreational property loans whenever the slightest trend toward foreclosure might be evident. Insurance companies can be equally stubborn about their rates and even their acceptance of properties which may be unoccupied much of the year, and therefore subject to many more risks due to vandalism, theft, and insufficient fire protection. The emotional desirability of a recreational property will also be influenced by seasonal variations that will intensify demand at one time of the year and cause it to fade at other times. Timing can therefore be critically important in attempting to either buy or sell recreational property. Despite changing economic conditions, one of the obvious drawbacks in searching for a personal recreational property is the realization that *old* money and *big* money has been used to obtain and control the choicest spots relative to large-population areas. The

---

*Chapter 5—"How to Accurately Assess the Value of a Property"; Chapter 6—"Buying Income-Producing Property at the Best Price"; and Chapter 7—"Conventional and Creative Ways to Finance Real Estate."

potential for acquiring under-valued or of finding the "hidden value" recreational property is therefore greatly reduced. Even the recreational lot which is held for construction of a residential dwelling at some time in the reasonable near future may be adversely affected by rapid changes in environmental law, new zoning restrictions, and so on. Careful research of many factors must be done before property acquisitions are made. The recommended techniques for conducting that research are described in the next few chapters.

5

How to Accurately Assess the Value of a Property

The recommended method of real-property analysis or assessment is the one used by professional appraisers—a multifactoral approach which effectively utilizes current and historical data to arrive at a reliable approximation of current market value. These various methods should be simultaneously considered *before* making any written commitment to buy *or* sell. To arrive at the "current market value," or "fair market value," there are at least nine methods of determining real-property value that must be understood and carefully applied to assure success with real-property investments. These various interrelated methods should be applied quickly and systematically each and every time an income-producing property is seriously being considered. The suggested methods that are most valid when used in combination are as follows:

1. Analysis* of the asking price, seller's motivation, and the original acquisition price
2. Analysis of current and previous tax assessment and rationale
3. Analysis of total income *vs.* total expenses (*e.g.*, "Annual Property Operating Data")**

---

*The term "analysis" is used here to suggest that the investor must be prepared to independently *think* about the significance of multiple bits of information relative to personal goals and capabilities.

**Reprinted with permission of the ®REALTORS NATIONAL MARKETING INSTITUTE® of the NATIONAL ASSOCIATION OF REALTORS® 1975. All rights reserved.

4. Analysis of square footage and additional amenities
5. Analysis of location, visual appeal, and desirability
6. Analysis of comparable values and/or sales
7. Analysis of broad economic factors
8. Analysis of terms relative to cost and rate of projected return
9. Analysis of buyer motivation, needs, and capabilities

1. Analysis of the Asking Price, Seller's Motivation, and the Original Acquisition Price

One of the most basic definitions of an economic transaction is the meeting ground that is established between the lowest point at which a seller is willing to part with something and the highest point at which a buyer is willing to acquire that thing. In the routine application of real-property transactions, there are distinct psychological elements that exist which often create an approach-avoidance conflict.* The seller usually feels that the property should have been sold for *more,* and the buyer feels that the property should have been acquired for *less!* This strong, mutually opposed emotion will contribute to the "killing" of many transactions which are not thoroughly put together and expediently handled.

The logical first step in evaluating the "true" value of any property is to obtain and use the "asking" price as a superficial criterion of the approximate price at which the seller will relinquish control of a particular property. Unrealistically low prices are scarce, even in an inflationary economy, and must be acted upon quickly. Accurately priced properties must be evaluated in terms of reliably meeting the investor's expectations. Unrealistically overpriced properties can be dangerous to one's financial health and warrant little more than a casual, one-time-only offer that is at least within reason. The "good tax shelter" that can be created by the overpriced property will typically not compensate for the higher risk in controlling the property and the lower potential resale value in the near future.

---

*In having intensely mixed positive and negative feelings about something, the more closely a person comes to that "thing," the more intense the negative feelings become. History and courtrooms are littered with persons who wanted to "back out" of contractual agreements.

ONE MORE FOOL THEORY

The underlying assumption of the "one more fool theory" is that, regardless of the price, someone will come along who will eventually pay *even more!* The key concept behind this theory is the term "eventually." The rampages of persistent inflation make this assumption valid whenever the buyer is willing to hold an overpriced property long enough.* One available means of assessing whether or not you are being considered a "financial pigeon" is to ask (or find out through county records) the year in which the property was acquired and then promptly go in person to the county records office, obtain the proper property identification number, and look up the available assessment records and the microfische records of the deed or mortgage on the concerned property. This virtually no-cost activity will allow you to verify the exact date of acquisition by the current owners, possible frequency of the recent turnovers (by previous book and page numbers), and the actual amount paid by the current sellers. Once you've obtained this *fundamental* information, in addition to the asking price and probable terms, you can ask yourself a number of questions, such as the following:

1. How much is the seller adding to the original purchase price?**
2. How much of this added "equity" is the result of improvements? Exclude the cost of repairs—the I.R.S. does.
3. How much actual inflation has there been since the property was last acquired?
4. How much capital gains tax, after commissions (if any), will the seller likely have to pay? Is an installment sale possible?
5. How much *more* could you reasonably expect to sell the property for in one year? Two years? Three? Try to discover more than the superficial reasons why the seller wants to sell. Obtain the seller's rationale and/or possible verification of the current market value of the property.

---

*This is especially true of non-income-producing land purchases.
**A good point to remember is that the original purchase price was the full market price that was agreed upon at the time of the original sale. It is quite possible that the sale price was unrealistically high at that time.

2. Analysis and Justification for Current and Previous Tax Assessment

Most counties are lawfully obligated to assess all taxable real property at some percentage (usually expressed as mills per thousand) of the estimated total value (usually approximating 100%). The rationale for determination of the assessed value is typically based on a combination of factors, such as the previous tax rate, age of the building, last purchase price, obvious improvements, current income from the property, and comparable sales and/or assessments. This property tax becomes a fixed expense which should be reasonably valid, but may or may not be. It can be reasonably predicted that the property taxes will increase each year unless some possible tax relief is legislated, such as Proposition 13, which has directly contributed to the establishment of rent controls in Los Angeles and other areas within California. Each area will have a basic rule of thumb that can be applied in computing the purchase price on the basis of the current tax assessment. This is one of the areas where your *own* personal real estate broker can be most helpful in discussing and evaluating how closely various properties are selling relative to their assessed values. There are always differences from one part of a local community to another on this ratio of assessed valuation to the actual selling price. Along these same lines there is another indirect method of determining "true value" which can be obtained from public tax assessment records. In most areas a city business license is required with any income-producing property of four or more units. This assessment is actually just another tax which is based upon a small percentage of the adjusted gross annual income. This raw data is part of the public domain and can be looked up and computed to determine what the actual ("conservative," not puffed up) adjusted annual income was for the previously reported tax year. This data can be especially useful when it is known that the property in question was owned by the same party throughout the previous tax year and when the approximate tax bracket of the owners can be reasonably estimated. Despite the illusion of friendliness, most are *not* going to compromise their privacy by showing the buyer a certified copy of their actual I.R.S. reports. When there is a high apparent risk or substantial sum of money involved in a particular transaction, a buyer can seek some additional protection by insisting upon a "Certified True Income and Expense Statement."

3. Analysis of Total Income vs. Total Expenses ("Annual Property Operating Data")

The traditional numerical method of assessing property value is to follow an established format such as the Annual Property Operating Data form. This worksheet can be ordered directly from REALTORS NATIONAL MARKETING INSTITUTE®, 430 North Michigan Avenue, Chicago, Illinois 60611. Similar forms can also be ordered or obtained from legal-stationery supply offices, and most real estate brokers' offices. This basic format can be quickly applied to each investment property under consideration until it becomes "natural" to compare one property against another. It is especially important that the other basic methods suggested in this chapter be used in conjunction with this basic form. One of the distinct advantages of this traditional worksheet document is that it will flag your attention to virtually all of the income and expense items that are critical in each transaction. The completed form will allow you to relate this raw data to the asking sale price, suggested down payment, and the various recommended terms as they relate to a particular investment "opportunity." The satisfaction that you have in reaching that privately desired "bottom line" will be very much reflected by the amount of verification you do of the individual items. Use every available resource to cross-reference and verify the information contained in a property-analysis form before making a final decision. The attached Annual Property Operating Data form regarding a sample single-family dwelling makes some references to capitalization rates (CAP rates) which will be an unfamiliar concept to many readers. A CAP rate is essentially the calculated percent of return after substracting all operating expenses from the assumed gross income. It is the percent of return, such as 6%, 7%, 8%, 9%, or fraction thereof, that local investors consider to be a "typical" return for a certain classification of property and within a local economic community. The CAP rate on single-family dwellings however is not especially valid and reliable because of the higher ratio of property value to actual income and the high variability in setting and receiving the "right" amount of monthly rent on that dwelling. One vacancy, for instance, in a single-family dwelling represents a 100% vacancy factor. This does not compare favorably with a 20-unit apartment complex in which one vacancy represents a 5% vacancy factor. The local "community of investors" will basically determine what the CAP rate in that area will be. This is done by averaging the actual CAP rates of a large number of investment properties to arrive at a local rule-of-thumb CAP rate such as 8.1% or 9.2%, etc. Knowledge of this going rate of return can assist the investor in quickly deciding how realistic a given sale price may be. When the CAP rate goes down from this norm, the value (perhaps merely the cost) goes up. The opposite is true as the CAP rate goes up. The investor who intends to make the best possible use of these shortcut forms must be constantly aware of the fact that errors in computation of the true income and true expenses (in the *next* twelve months) will significantly distort the true current market value of the property.

4. Analysis of Square Footage and Additional Amenities

Real estate "experts" such as local municipal building authorities, established building contractors, public and private property appraisors, commercial lending institutions, insurance agents, and real estate brokers all tend to subscribe to authoritative periodicals which allow them to quickly establish a fairly reliable index of the cost per square foot for most types of new construction.* Wood-frame construction, for instance, may be

---
*Example: *Building Standards: The National Magazine for Building Officials,* International Conference of Building Officials, 5360 South Workman Mill Road, Wittier, Calif. 90601.

Annual Property Operating Data

Date: January 15, 1980
Price: $ 52,000
Loans: $ 39,375
Equity: $ 12,625

Purpose: Seller desires larger property
Name: *****
Location: 13409 S. E. Stark St. Seattle, Wn.
Type of Property: Ranch style residential house

Assessed/Appraised Values
- Land: $ 10,000 — 21 %
- Improvement: $ 35,775 — 75 %
- Personal Property: $ 2,000 — 04 %
- Total: $ 47,775 — 100 %
- Adjusted Basis as of *****: $ ____

FINANCING

	Balance	Payment	# Pymt/Yr.	Interest	Term
Existing 1st	$ 25,400	204.50	2,454	8.5 %	25
2nd	$ 13,975	135.10	1,621	10.0 %	20
3rd	$			%	
Potential 1st	$			%	
2nd	$			%	

		%	2	3	Comments
1	SCHEDULED RENTAL INCOME 450/mo	100		5,400.00	Three bedrooms & two
2	Less: Vacancy and Credit Losses	.05		270.00	baths in older brick
3	EFFECTIVE RENTAL INCOME	.95		5,130.00	home with large living
4	Plus: Other Income	—			room, dining room,
5	GROSS OPERATING INCOME	.95		5,130.00	kitchen & double garage.
6	Less: Operating Expenses				
7	Accounting and Legal	.01	51.00		Projected negative cash
8	Advertising, Licenses and Permits	.03	154.00		flow suggests increased
9	Property Insurance	.04	205.00		risk factor. Careful
10	Property Management	—			analysis recommended.
11	Payroll—Resident Management	—			Potential tax shelter
12	Other	—			very good. Potential
13	Taxes—Worker's Compensation	—			to upgrade income and
14	Personal Property Taxes	—			appreciation also very
15	Real Estate Taxes	.23	1,180.00		good.
16	Repairs and Maintenance	.05	257.00		
17	Services—Elevator	—			
18	Janitorial	—			CAP = NOI / Sale Price
19	Lawn	—			
20	Pool	—			CAP = $3,026 / $52,000
21	Rubbish	.02	103.00		
22	Other	—			CAP = 6 Percent
23	Supplies	.01	51.00		
24	Utilities—Electricity	—			A sample depreciation
25	Gas and Oil	—			schedule:
26	Sewer and Water	.02	103.00		Improvement @ $40,000
27	Telephone	—			with s/l @ 20 yrs life
28	Other	—			$40,000 x .05 = $2,000
29	Miscellaneous	—			Personal prop. @ $2,000
30					with s/l @ 5 yrs life
31	TOTAL OPERATING EXPENSES	.41		2,104.00	$2,000 x .20 = $400
32	NET OPERATING INCOME	.59		3,026.00	Annual depreciation =
33	Less: Annual Debt Service			4,075.00	$2,400. Taxes, interest &
34	CASH FLOW BEFORE TAXES			-1,049.00	expenses are also deductable.

NATIONAL ASSOCIATION OF REALTORS®
developed in cooperation with its affiliate, the
REALTORS NATIONAL MARKETING INSTITUTE®
1975. 3-79-F601

The statements and figures presented herein, while not guaranteed, are secured from sources we believe authoritative.

Prepared by Jay M. Kimmel

Note to Cornerstone LIBRARY: See required footnote annotation from R.N.M.I. p. 106

Reprinted with permission of the ®REALTORS NATIONAL MARKETING INSTITUTE® of the NATIONAL ASSOCIATION OF REALTORS®. 1975. All rights reserved.

Annual Property Operating Data

Date: February 6, 1980
Price: $105,600
Loans: $65,000
Equity: $40,600

Purpose: Liquidation
Name: Eucalyptus Apartments
Location: 4312 - 4318 Powell Blvd. Oakland
Type of Property: Two-story, wood-frame, 4-plex
Assessed/Appraised Values:
- Land: $18,270 — 20 %
- Improvement: $65,080 — 71 %
- Personal Property: $8,000 — 09 %
- Total: $91,350 — 100 %

Adjusted Basis as of _____ $ _____

FINANCING

	Balance	Payment	# Pymt/Yr.	Interest	Term
Existing 1st	$47,000	378.18	4,538	9.0 %	30 yrs
2nd	$18,000	179.71	2,157	10.5 %	20 yrs
3rd				%	
Potential 1st				%	
2nd				%	

#		%	2	3	Comments
1	SCHEDULED RENTAL INCOME $300/mo	1.00		14,400.00	Four two-bedroom units.
2	Less: Vacancy and Credit Losses	.03		432.00	Includes w/w carpeting,
3	EFFECTIVE RENTAL INCOME	.98		13,968.00	draperies & all electric
4	Plus: Other Income Laundry room $25/mo	.02		300.00	appliances. This nine
5	GROSS OPERATING INCOME	.99		14,268.00	year old 4-plex has been
6	Less: Operating Expenses				recently remodeled; has
7	Accounting and Legal	.01	143		ample off-street parking
8	Advertising, Licenses and Permits	.05	713		and is near public trans-
9	Property Insurance	.04	571		portation and shopping.
10	Property Management	—			
11	Payroll-Resident Management (discount)	.02	285		
12	Other	—			
13	Taxes-Worker's Compensation	—			
14	Personal Property Taxes	.20	2,854		Sample depreciation:
15	Real Estate Taxes	.05	713		
16	Repairs and Maintenance	—			Improvement @ $82,600
17	Services-Elevator	—			with s/l @ 20 yrs life
18	Janitorial	—			$82,600 x .05 = $4,130
19	Lawn	—			Personal prop. @ $8,000
20	Pool	—			with s/l @ 6 yrs life
21	Rubbish (drop box)	.01	143		$8,000 x .17 = $1,333
22	Other	—			Annual deprec. = $5,463
23	Supplies	.01	143		
24	Utilities-Electricity (laundry rm., etc.)	.01	143		Projected income = $14,268
25	Gas and Oil	—			Projected expenses, deprec-
26	Sewer and Water	.03	428		iation & interest = $17,892
27	Telephone	—			Net "loss" = $3,624
28	Other	—			
29	Miscellaneous	—			Projected gain =
30					a. Small equity growth
31	TOTAL OPERATING EXPENSES	.43		6,136.00	b. Good appreciation
32	NET OPERATING INCOME	.57		8,133.00	c. Tax shelter
33	Less: Annual Debt Service	—		6,695.00	d. Positive cash flow
34	CASH FLOW BEFORE TAXES	—		+1,438.00	

NATIONAL ASSOCIATION OF REALTORS®
developed in cooperation with its affiliate, the
REALTORS NATIONAL MARKETING INSTITUTE®
1975. 3-79-F501

The statements and figures presented herein, while not guaranteed, are secured from sources we believe authoritative.

Prepared by: Jay M. Kimmel

Ibid., p. 106

Reprinted with permission of the ®REALTORS NATIONAL MARKETING INSTITUTE® of the NATIONAL ASSOCIATION OF REALTORS®. 1975. All rights reserved.

estimated at $30 per square foot in one area and $60 per square foot in another. Style, location, and a wide range of amenities will significantly influence the cost per square foot. Concrete or aggregate block construction will be slightly and perhaps substantially more per square foot. Established and reliable builders can estimate the costs per square foot on the basis of their own recent experience in the local economy. Such builders typically maintain regular contact with similar construction companies in the area and can often benefit from the other companies' experience in calculating the actual costs for a particular type of dwelling. Among investors with an interest in new construction, the likely preference would be for dwellings that are essentially built for long- or short-term lease purposes. "Custom-built" dwellings will rarely be practical for conversion to rental units, unless perhaps only a brief interval is anticipated before the units are converted to condominiums or cooperatives. A cluster of quality built duplexes, for example, might be later converted to co-op or condo ownership. In general, most multiple units will be designed and constructed for rental, co-op, or condominium purposes only and will be much more cost effective per square foot than private, single-family dwellings would be.

The "replacement costs" per square foot that are used as guidelines by local insurance agents are also reasonable criteria to quickly evaluate the appropriateness of a given asking price. It is often easy to obtain the square footage from the seller, the seller's agent (if any), and, as a matter of habit, from the county tax assessment records. By simply multiplying the appropriate local cost per square foot times the verified square footage, a very reliable, "rule of thumb," quantitative value can be established as *one* of the many criteria for determining an accurate value for a particular property. It should be kept in mind that insurance company estimates of replacement costs are for the building only, not the land. Land values should be independently determined in the same manner to establish a reasonable cost per square foot in a particular locale. The simple procedure is to multiply this guideline by the total square footage of the lot, or land, etc., and add this amount to the estimated figures for the building. The determination of the value of the land at a particular building site is not the same method that can be applied to determine the "allocation" between the total value of the land and the building for depreciation and income tax purposes.* Other adjustments will have to be made as appropriate with any number of potential amenities which are above and beyond the absolute minimum in expected circumstances and services. "View" property, for instance, will always have a higher prestige and desirability value and yet not make increased demands upon the owner/manager. A swimming pool, however, will add value but will also bring with it complex liability issues, safety issues, and maintenance issues which cannot be neglected. Some amenities, such as a swimming pool, could have a negative economic value by taking up needed off-street parking spaces. The flat, two-dimensional space which exists on a plot map may in reality have critical access problems, extreme steepness, or extreme shallowness which impairs the economic and physical use of the land. A substantial argument can be made for personally inspecting any real property before making a commitment to acquire it. Numerous are the buyers who made legal commitments to purchase "bargain-priced" real property which turned out to be inaccessible, eroding tidal flats, swamplands, gullies, desert, rocky escarpments, and so on. Much personal judgment must be exercised in making a decision to purchase real property by the square foot.

5. Analysis of Location, Visual Appeal, and Desirability

Location, visual appeal, and desirability are the most intangible, non-numerical qualities of an income-producing property which are critical factors for maximal income development, future appreciation, and economy of resale. These essentially subjective characteristics will be a test of your personal judgment in assessing what is "attractive" and "desirable" to other people. The test is not so much how the property appeals to you person-

---

*See section on estimating values for depreciation purposes in Chapter 1.

ally, but more importantly what the realistic potential is to positively appeal to others—month-to-month renters, as well as the future buyer. Is the location of the property appropriate and compatible with the long-range intention of providing residential rental space? Is the area free from aversive sights and conditions that would detract from the goal of providing comfortable and healthful residential space? Is the area free from aversive changes that could likely occur in the near future?

There is an inescapable trace of logic in the frequently heard, if not trite expression, that, "The three most important factors in any real estate purchase are location, location, and location!" Aside from the chuckle that this expression sometimes brings, a favorable location will significantly enhance the appreciation of an income-producing property. The exact definition of "favorable location" is interpreted by contemporary group consensus more than it is by established norms. Favorable location can refer to an economically desirable area, compatibility with other dwellings, high visibility, ease of locating, proximity to desirable resources, freedom from aversive sights, sounds, other undesirable conditions, and so on. If there was a prolonged gasoline shortage, favorable location could refer to the geographically convenient or "close in" properties. If energy sources in general experience prolonged shortages, favorable location could refer to the more temperate climate zones in the world. As the worldwide "economics of scarcity" becomes more and more of a personal reality, it becomes even more important to concentrate upon favorable locations, verify all financial data, verify vacancy rates, and avoid gross over-extension of your own resources.

Visual appeal will consistently be very important in establishing that critical first impression on the prospective tenant that tends to occur in the first few seconds after locating and observing a potential future residence for the first time. Ultimately, it is this same "first impression" that will be critical in establishing a positive image for prospective buyers who will eventually be asked to pay much more for the same dwelling site (assuming adjustments for improvements, inflation, and other miscellaneous "profit") than you originally paid for the property. Physical attractiveness of the property should be a major concern of the investor. You can effectively appeal to a prospective buyer's emotions by appropriately upgrading the property. As a general rule, exhibit a lot of building, not a lot of vegetation. Remove or improve upon physical barriers or obstacles that could detract from the total dwelling. Install substantial and attractive front doors and improve upon the entranceways in particular to facilitate that critical first-impression process. Study the potential cosmetic improvements, especially landscaping of the building site, which can be improved upon to give the impression of being clean, orderly, well maintained, and "attractive to others." On the basis of that critical first impression, most persons will try to subjectively answer the question: "What will my friends and family think of me if I should live here, or if I should buy this particular dwelling?"

6. Analysis of Comparable Values and/or Sales

One of the best rules of thumb for assessing the value of a particular property is to validate the actual sale price of similar or "comparable" properties in the same general vicinity. This is one of the major techniques utilized by licensed, professional property appraisers. Their methods of determining current market values (for whatever reason: sale, probate, legal dispute, etc.) *must* be valid even if challenged in a court of law. In contrast, licensed real estate personnel use their "professional judgment" to render similar (and often highly accurate) determinations of value; however, their opinions would not ordinarily stand up in a court of law, and are directly influenced by the desire to obtain a contractual listing. The consequential process of considering offers and counter-offers (if any) will supposedly rectify an overly optimistic total sale price plus commission. The licensed appraisor, on the other hand, provides a limited service for a specific fee and would generally be lacking in any other vested interest in the property. Licensed appraisers have been extensively and formally trained and experienced in this one specific aspect of the entire real estate field. They consistently provide a detailed and thorough report that can be cross-validated by others, if necessary. In addition to making a thorough on-site inspection and of making a precise inventory, measurements, and a floor plan, the professional appraiser usually retains a clerical staff that routinely researches governmental property records, title records, etc. These "clerks" are thoroughly experienced in researching county records to obtain a maximum amount of usable data. This data will also include detailed summaries of the recent history of property sales in the area to establish a sample of properties which are similar with respect to type, total square footage, similar amenities, and so on, and in a rather detailed and systematic fashion. Proportionately, by skipping the independent professional research and advice to save either time or money, the non-consultant investor often makes very costly errors in value judgments. The investor, for instance, who refuses to consider a $125 appraisal fee—only ¼ of 1% of a $50,000 purchase or sale price—could be wasting thousands!

7. Analysis of Broad Economic Factors

There are a number of economic indices which the income property investor must maintain an ongoing awareness of. The basic indices would typically include such economic factors as:

   a. Analysis of current interest rates. Up? Down? Stable?
   b. Analysis of current inflation rates. Reliably up? Down? Stable?
   c. Analysis of current availability of money. Scarce? Expensive? Private?
   d. Analysis of current monthly mortgage payments. Full amortization? Interest only?
   e. Analysis of current vacancy rates. Verifiable? Trend? Concessions?
   f. Analysis of current construction rates. Over-production? Slow selling?
   g. Analysis of current default and bankrupty rates. Gov't. and lender statistics.
   h. Analysis of current unemployment rates. Potential or *real* recession?

i. Analysis of current stocks-and-bond returns. Movement toward? Away from?
j. Analysis of current gold, oil, gem, and collector markets. Up? Down? Stable?
k. Analysis of current consumer preferences and population trends. Rising demand?
l. Analysis of current net income *vs.* basic necessities. Up? Down? Stable?
m. Analysis of current property income *vs.* total expenses. Positive cash flow?

Unless there is a drastic and enduring change in one or more of the areas indicated above, it will generally be sufficient to assess the overall *trends* of these broad indicators of economic change in making your own investment projections for the near future. The indispensable input of investor newsletters,* quality newspapers, relevant textbooks, and journals,** and other media reports of economic and social conditions, will invariably assist the attentive investor in remaining well ahead of the "masses" with respect to economic planning and decision-making. Investment strategies must always be responsive to changing conditions. The low liquidity of real estate in general obligates the real-property investor to concentrate more on current and near future economics and to avoid making the classic error of casually buying the wrong property and then either holding it indefinitely until there is a significant improvement in value, or until the property is owned free and clear. It's all right for an investor to create the impression of being impulsive, but in reality the most successful investors will actually be very quick about doing the required "homework"; be knowledgeable about the broad economic market, and quick to insert "qualifiers" in any written agreements for areas which have not yet been researched to the satisfaction of the investor.

---

*"Real Estate Investing Letter," United Media International, Inc., 306 Dartmouth Street, Boston, Mass. 02116 ($35 per year); and: "Apartment Management Newsletter," 48 W. 21st Street, New York, N.Y. 10010 ($48 per year).

**Real Estate Review, Warren, Gorham & Lamont, 210 South Street, Boston, Mass. 02111 ($34 per year); published quarterly.

8. Analysis of Terms Relative to Cost and Rate of Projected Return

Most income properties would now suffer a lower degree of appreciation if they were sold on the basis of net income only. The reason for this is that expenses have increased at rates that are significantly higher than rental rates have increased. Utilities, taxes, materials and supplies, labor, and all other expenses connected with income-producing properties have been steadily increasing at rates which are much higher than would be customarily allowed to occur with rental increases. Rents have become a bargain in the pre-rent-control market in which new apartment construction has been substantially discouraged because first-owner investors are unable to avoid a substantial negative cash flow in the first year or two after completion within the existing rental market. New apartment complexes don't "pencil out," that is, realistic net income for such properties typically will not cover the debt service unless "highly unusual" arrangements for financing can be made. The conservative institutional lenders are looking for *at least* a 1.2 cover before even considering a loan. In other words, the realistic net income must provide at least 120% of the total debt service. Many of the "good tax shelter deals" on the market today have a reversed ratio of income to debt service. The realistic net income may be providing only 80% of the total debt service, and the balance must come from some other source! Under such circumstances, new apartment construction tends to be limited to individuals and corporations with reliably high annual incomes where a portion of that income can be plowed back into the complex in return for the "advantages" of creative accelerated depreciation and hopefully strong, future appreciation. Anyone else buying such a property would run the risk of having to make up that monthly deficit from uncertain, and perhaps *very expensive,* sources.

A few years ago it would have been unreasonable, perhaps unthought of, to seriously consider paying 8, 10, and even 12 or more times the *gross* annual income for a multiple-unit apartment building. Such a high-gross multiplier would appear to be especially ludicrous in the case of certain apartments in which central heating and all utilities are paid for by the owner! The more "sophisticated" method of the recent past (and actually of the present) was to estimate the value of an income-producing property by *dividing* the realistic net income by the desired capitalization (CAP) rate. The typically desirable CAP rate for apartment complexes in most communities would be an obtainable fraction between 8% and 12%. This method is relatively crude, but it does allow the investor to seek certain ratios of indebtedness to income which will provide a definable return. An investor who wants a 9% return on a $50,000 loan would have to show a net operating income of $4,500. The variability in this method of predicting outcomes is that the $50,000 loan could be financed under any number of different interest rates and other terms. Two different investors could each have similar $50,000 houses which are each rented at $450 per month, and one investor could be receiving a strong positive cash flow and the other could be receiving a distinct negative cash flow. The CAP rate, like the gross multiplier, will not differentiate among the various interest rates and terms that are possible within even the same transaction by using the above method. The CAP rate as described above will help in establishing more realistic values for investment properties which have a poorer net operating income situation than the "gross multiplier method" ever would. For a more sophisticated CAP rate which actually incorporates the loan debt to value ratios, the interest rates, and the term of the loan (percent constant), *and* the cash flow, or debt coverage ratio in one neat little package, see the "Gettel Method" in Ronald E. Gettel's *Real Estate Guidelines and Rules of Thumb.*[*]

In the case of the Wildwood Apartments (hypothetical fourplex), the asking price was $80,000 and the realistic net income after the first twelve months was determined to be $9,336. By dividing the net income by the asking price, a CAP rate of 11.7% will be obtained. This is considered to be a desirable return of

---

[*]Gettel, Ronald E., *Real Estate Guidelines and Rules of Thumb,* New York: McGraw-Hill Book Company, 1976; pp. 132–39.

almost 12% purely on the ratio of total indebtedness to total income in the first year. The other benefits of ownership, such as cash flow, equity gain, tax shelter, and appreciation have not yet been computed into the total yield. The key benefit of establishing such a narrowly defined CAP rate is that the ratio of total indebtedness to total net income is more clearly emphasized as the quality of the net operating income declines. Example: if the total net operating income of the Wildwood Apartments was actually $6,800 at the end of the first twelve months, the CAP rate would be 8.5%, and the overall margin for control of the property and future profits could be seriously threatened at the current asking price of $80,000. The scenario becomes even worse (for most investors) as the asking price increases and the capitalization rate decreases. Stated another way, the lower the CAP rate, the higher (more risk) the gross multiplier. The substitute, of course, for attempting to match investment properties with a particular capitalization rate is carefully analyzing the income and expenses relative to the actual cost of the desired financing to determine the quality and reliability of a personally desirable cash flow. The investment property which cannot reasonably meet your expectations for a definable cash flow without over-embellished occupancy rates and promises of "unusual" potential to upgrade income should be assessed with much skepticism and a strong desire to consider *other* investment opportunities.

9. Analysis of Buyer Motivation, Needs, and Capabilities

The most subjective criteria for analysis of a property's inherent value are the psychological and personal motivations for buying a particular property at a particular time. The vagueness of the "unpredictable" economic future at the moment of making a legal commitment to acquire (and/or dispose of, in the case of an exchange) a real property will naturally be rather anxiety-provoking and unnerving. The buyer's aspirations, uncertainties, and questions must be suddenly converted to constructive actions. Major errors must be avoided. In wading through the final decisions about value related to indebtedness, upside potential, personal tax consequences, and so on, the knowledgeable investor as well as the beginner must rely upon a certain amount of primitive guesswork and intuitive judgment. That "little nudge" which stirs the investor to make tangible commitments in writing will be greatly enhanced by the suggested guidelines for fundamental property research, persistent inquisitiveness, and appropriate "in lieu of" qualifiers for all areas which have not been verified to the buyer's satisfaction in advance. It is through prompt and systematic research of a potential investment property, and the practice of assertively seeking answers to the "right" questions, that the necessary information for decision-making will usually present itself. A tested format for conducting a detailed analysis of a potential investment property *before* making a premature commitment is discussed in detail in the following chapter.

6

Buying Income-Producing Property at the Best Price

Once you have analyzed the relative and comparable values of a potential investment property ("by the numbers"), there are *other* variables which need to be analyzed to be assured that you can obtain a particular property "at the best price." The reliable method for doing this is to follow a checklist such as the two different types described in this chapter, or perhaps modified lists that you can develop and use for yourself. The recommended goal is to have a standardized procedure to follow for the rapid and thorough evaluation of potential income-producing properties. In making any large investment, it is quite often the questions which you failed to ask (or failed to obtain complete answers to) that will haunt you throughout the life of the particular investment. Following a "standardized" procedure of some type will also assist you greatly in making direct and accurate comparisons between one potential investment property and another. This is essentially the method that licensed property appraisors and licensed real estate brokers utilize in determining current market values. The "professionals" also rely heavily on records of "comparable sales," "builder's replacement costs," and intuitive judgments about the physical and economic desirability and attractiveness of a particular unit of real property. The "best price" for a potential investment property is not always the lowest possible price. A property does not have to be a "steal" to

Buying Income-Producing Property

eventually meet your specific investment objectives. The ti.. factors and the various degrees of success you will experience in meeting investment objectives depend largely on the quality and reliability of a particular property to economically perform in a fairly predictable manner and to have fairly predictable maintenance and other expenses. A well-analyzed property should meet most of your personal expectations. The time to do most or all of that analysis is *before* you commit yourself to an earnest money agreement which is at least potentially enforceable.* Make up a large supply of "inquiry forms" for personal worksheets and use them with each property to be analyzed as a potential investment.

INVESTOR'S INITIAL INQUIRY FORM

1. Date:_____ Date property first put on the market: _____

2. Address of property for sale: _____

3. Directions on how to find (if necessary):_____

   _____

4. Complete description as advertised, asking price, and source of information: _____

   _____

   _____

---

*The enforceability of the conventional earnest money agreement has been a subject for legal debate for at least the past 50 years. The issue is generally whether an earnest money agreement is a legally binding contract, or merely an "option" to purchase real property. Most brokers will argue (*cf.* bluff) that it is enforceable; most attorneys will say that *all* elements of a legally binding contract must be present and demonstrable, or it is not enforceable. A general rule from practice is that a well-written earnest money agreement is more binding on the seller to sell than on the buyer to buy. At any rate, obtaining a legal decision *after the fact* can be hard to predict, and expensive. As a buyer, *always* insert conditional clauses to create an "exit," if felt necessary.

5. Seller's name, address, and telephone (obtain through county records, if necessary): _____
_____

6. Seller's agent (if any) (name, address, and telephone): _____
_____

7. Stated reason for selling: _____
_____

8. Evaluation of neighborhood: _____
_____
_____
_____

9. Legal description:_____
10. Total sq. ft. of building:_____Average sq. ft. of rooms or units: _
11. Total sq. ft. of lot:_____Dimensions of lot:_____Paved road:_
12. County's assessed value:_____Taxes paid last year:
_____

13. Financial terms desired: _____Alternatives:

   a. Owner willing to carry contract:_____Percent down: _____
   b. Owner willing to make a tax-deferred exchange: _____
   Up/Down:_____
   c. Cash out plus assumption:_____Current balance: _____
   Interest:_____
   d. Consider FHA/VA:_____Willing to pay cost of discount points:_____
   e. Conventional financing only:_____Percent down: _____
   Interest:_____

14. Notes: _____

_____

_____

The following comments represent a brief item analysis of the questions contained in the Investor's Initial Inquiry Form:

1. Date

Timing is always a fairly crucial item in identifying, evaluating, and making decisions about potential investment property. On this sample form it is merely helpful to pinpoint exactly when you first became aware of a potential investment opportunity. It is also helpful to know how long a property has been on the market. If the property has been available for several weeks or longer, there may be some significant flaws which others have found and rejected (unrealistic price being a common flaw). Do your homework quickly and avoid being intimidated by time. Sellers and agents for sellers will typically want you to believe there are tangible buyers who are rushing around at this moment to obtain the necessary financing for the full asking price. Don't let such pressures influence your decision. It is financially better in the long run to miss out on a sure money-maker than it is to impetuously rush into a money-loser.

2. Address of Property for Sale

It is essential that you obtain the specific address of the property being offered at the very beginning of the inquiry and not just a general location. Don't give your name out to "just anyone" in exchange for the address. At the very least, find out who took the listing and deal only with that person. This alone will strengthen any offer you may subsequently make to the seller. You must know exactly which property is being offered so you can make a quick visual inspection of the property and its setting in the neighborhood or community before you are assailed by a sales agent's claims and an owner's fluff, e.g., "You probably won't find a better bargain anywhere in this neighborhood." A second and equally important reason to obtain the complete address is that this will give you the opportunity to rush to the county courthouse to quickly and inexpensively (usually no record charge) research the detailed assessment records, county appraisal information that supports a particular assessment, and actually look at copies of the current and recent deeds to know what was previously paid for the property, when it was paid, etc. You may then be prepared to submit an extensively qualified offer, a "ridiculous" offer, or reject the whole thing and move on to the next "opportunity."

3. Directions on How to Find

Unless it is completely obvious where a particular property is located, it is frequently useful to have someone else describe to you how they would go about locating the property in question. Some of the issues that you might mentally take note of might be such things as: "Is the property easily accessible?" "Is the property suitably located?" "Is the property on or near a main arterial?" "Is the property in an area of comparably priced buildings?" If the property is worth taking a second look at, consider taking alternate routes to get there; research the neighborhood for possible irritants such as railroad tracks or crossings, airport flight paths, major highway or interstate highway noises, dumping areas, commercial or industrial congestion, etc.

4. Complete Description as Advertised, Asking Price, and Source of Information

For a comparative evaluation after you have inspected the property yourself, it may be useful to have a concise description of how the owner or the sales agent "saw" the property being offered. This initial statement should contain most or all of the positive selling features of the potential investment property. If you first discover the property from an ad in the newspaper, copy the ad verbatim. Also, copy all information taken over the phone as you are preparing to "drive up" on your own and to perhaps schedule an appointment for a tour of the property and additional information. You can later judge for yourself just how much of the original advertising was distorted or perhaps just non-accountable seller's fluff. If the price is not listed in the ad, it is most helpful to at least obtain the "asking price" during this initial inquiry. Finally, you will want to differentiate between the parties who are attempting to make the sale themselves and their designated sales agent. In the case of the latter, it is very important to determine who obtained the original listing before you give out your own name. To a lesser extent, it may be helpful to determine if the listing is new, exclusive, or taken from the multiple listings. A multiple listing will usually tell you that the property has been around for a while and could not be successfully encumbered or sold by the agent and/or broker who took the original listing. In some instances you may want to call your *own* broker to verify the type of listing and how long it's been on the market.

5. Seller's Name, Address, and Telephone

It is generally quite important to know exactly who the actual owners of an advertised or interesting property happen to be. You cannot verify the most recent deed of record unless you are relatively certain of the legal owners' names. An investor should not be making serious offers to purchase real property when it is not known when the seller purchased the property and the amount paid. Also, in transactions which are being handled by agents for the owner, such as out-of-state owners, corporations, or highly private and confidential owners, you may be at a distinct disadvantage in your evaluation of the property without some direct input from the actual owners. Agents for the seller are typically well-trained sales staff who will do their best to "sell" you on a particular property. Sales agents often possess much knowledge of comparable properties and the closing of basically uncomplicated transactions. Otherwise, the sales agent basically knows only what the seller reveals about the property and enough to complete a sketchy listing agreement. The seller and/or the designated agent are rarely redressed for minor transgressions, misrepresentation, or errors of omission—unless the responsible parties are held accountable in writing for detailed claims about the property. The random agent who insists upon "protecting" the owner's right to privacy in disclosing precise and thorough information about the property is possibly hoping that you will drop your questions as being somehow inappropriate and that you will either buy or not buy the property without making anyone too accountable for specific facts about the property.

6. Seller's Agent (Name, Address and Telephone)

Most of the time you will be working directly with an agent who has obtained a contractual agreement to represent the seller and to contribute his or her particular expertise to the selling process. At all times the seller's agent is obligated by law to represent only the seller (fiduciary relationship), and irregardless of the amount of sincerity, politeness, or helpfulness, the seller's agent cannot equally represent the interests of the seller and the buyer. Buyers and sellers of real property can be considered to be involved in an adversary relationship, and real estate agents are strictly on the side of the person with whom they can obtain a contractual agreement. As an investor, you should make an early effort to obtain information about the name, address, telephone number, and *background* of the real estate agent involved and determine how much assistance this individual may be able to provide for you. Some sales agents have had substantial experience in the investment field and may be either directly or incidentally willing to provide useful information in evaluating the potential of a current investment property or perhaps similar ones. The same agent may be aware of or represent several comparable properties and be able to help you to differentiate among them. Don't be lulled to sleep by an agent who is ethically bound to strictly represent the interests of someone else. Place your trust in yourself, your personally selected real estate broker, your own attorney, and other professionals whose services *you* are paying for.

7. Stated Reason for Selling

The stated reason for selling is in all probability only the convenient reason for selling. The owner is moving to another state. The owner is retiring. The owner is looking for something different, etc. The business world (*i.e.*, real estate) is too multifaceted for such simplistic explanations. Just consider, for instance, the multiple reasons why you brush your teeth each day. The prevention of cavities is only one of many different possible reasons. To utilize the perspective of an investor, you should be very attentive to the covert reasons that a property is suddenly being marketed. In today's market you might be especially cautious about any proposition which offers a positive cash flow. With the pressures of inflationary prices, your new basis and "position" in a property at the full asking price could change a profitable investment into a substantial liability. When the sales agent is predominantly emphasizing the potential for tax shelter and the reliability of a zero-vacancy factor, or "upside" potential with some upgrading, be especially cautious. The present market of highly mobile tenants may not respond well to the new, proposed rent schedule. The margin for error is less for the new owner because of the entirely new basis in the property. Under the proposed new circumstances, it may be difficult to duplicate the experience of the current seller. Protect yourself by gathering all of the factual information about the property that you reasonably can. Look up recent mortgage and deed records. Analyze for yourself the significance of either frequent or infrequent turnover. Analyze the tax consequences of the seller. Critically think about the manner and means with which you could market that same property in the near future.

8. Evaluation of the Neighborhood

The old "drive by" method of appraising real estate does have its shortcomings. Too much reliance can be placed on that quick, initial impression of the exterior of a building and its immediate surroundings. By training yourself to do more than just "drive by," you can effectively compare and evaluate many potential investment properties without the intimacy of an appointment with a sales agent and a guided tour. Evaluation of a particular dwelling and the surrounding neighborhood can begin with a casual review of the surrounding buildings, roads, and general state of the economic development in the immediate community. The internal consistency or inconsistency of the neighborhood will tell you some things about the enforcement of the basic zoning requirements and perhaps whether the surrounding neighborhood is in a state of economic stability, ascent, or decline. More specific inquiries might be made if you were the least bit uncertain or suspicious. Neighbors and nearby vendors may be familiar with the property and willing to enter into a little casual conversation. Other leads might come from a real estate broker or real estate loan officer in the area who could tell you something about the economic history of that particular area. The local neighborhood association or even the chamber of commerce may be able to provide some additional information. Your own broker may know something about the investment potential in that particular area. Utility companies, mail carriers, and other service vendors may be able to help you in piecing together an occupancy (or vacancy) history in that neighborhood.

Another strategy is to spend a bit of your time observing what happens at different times during the day and evening. Park your car on the street nearby and observe what happens during the rush hour in the evening. Assess the street lighting and parking patterns after dark and late at night. Be attentive to possible irritants such as traffic or commercial noise, overcrowded conditions in the neighborhood, or any possible distraction which might have an adverse effect upon tenant satisfaction with the area. Try to assess the general age and income level of the residents in the neighborhood by estimating the value of the nearby dwellings, the value of the automobiles, the style of dress of the residents, and the general "life-style." Neighborhoods seem to attract basically similar residents. An apartment building which is mostly occupied by young persons can rarely be converted to a residence for seniors without a good deal of trauma. Middle-income persons will avoid a conspicuously lower-income neighborhood. Rentals which are near a college campus can be subject to very high vacancy rates during the summer months. Rentals which draw their residents from one particular industry in the community can be profoundly hurt in a recession that effects that industry. Neighborhoods which are marked by neglect and in a state of downward transition can be areas of concentrated crime, or places where the fear of crime will have a detrimental effect on prospective and current tenants. The absence of convenient shopping (especially for groceries) or other common community resources will also have a detrimental effect upon tenants. A phrase that you will often hear in connection with any real estate is that the three most important characteristics of a good investment property are—location, location, and location!

9. Legal Description

There are a number of reasons for wanting to obtain a complete and accurate legal description of any property in which you have more than a passing interest. Occasionally a legal description will be very long and contain information about peculiarities such as unusual metes and bounds or other lot dimensions. For purposes of verifying the current and past tax assessments (and the accompanying rationale), it is important to be sure that you have identified the correct property. With a correct legal description you can gather the necessary information to look up the county's record of mortgages and deeds to obtain specific information about previous prices paid, dates of sale, current owner, etc. Another quick screening technique is to call the "customer service" unit of a local title company and ask for the current property tax assessment of a property which you can then identify with the correct legal description. These and similar records are essentially part of the public domain and should be seriously considered for use by the investor as well as the experienced real estate personnel. You must avoid being shy or reluctant to use information that can be obtained through public records. A typical real estate investor will pay out far more in property taxes than the average property owner. Investors, therefore, support a good portion of the "legalistic" property record-keeping systems in each county. Originally, the purpose of these various record-keeping systems and the establishment of formal legal descriptions was to minimize disputes over the true ownership and boundaries when two or more parties got together with the intent of buying, selling, or exchanging land.

10. Total Square Footage of the Building, Average Square Footage of the Rooms or Units

One of the major determinants of sale value and rental value is the total square footage of a residential dwelling. For obvious reasons there are often intentional or unintentional "errors" in quoting the actual amount of usable square footage in each individual dwelling. The seller and/or his/her designated agent often record a "visual impression" of the square footage involved, or perhaps measure the external dimensions of the building quite liberally (front and side), multiplies the figures together, and gives a distorted impression of the amount of livable or rentable space which may be available. Such casual measurements can significantly inflate the assumed value of a particular building, and de-emphasize the unusable space, such as poorly placed walls, alcoves, oversized entrances and hallways, disproportionate room sizes, illegal room sizes, ceilings too low, etc. Before making a serious offer, you may want to obtain precise figures about the measurements of the building. It is quite possible that the seller or the seller's agent has exaggerated figures. At an appropriate time, this more carefully obtained information can be tactfully presented to the seller along with the request that the price be adjusted to reflect the more accurate square footage.

New construction costs and fire insurance rates are frequently computed on a cost-per-square-foot basis. Example: with a new single-family dwelling with 2,400 square feet and a cost estimate of $34 per square foot of construction, the selling price would be set at approximately $81,600 (2,400 × $34) for the building and perhaps $40,000 for the lot for a total sale price of $121,600. Insurance agents periodically contact property owners to remind them that the cost of new construction has increased and therefore the existing square footage should be insured at a higher valuation (and a higher premium rate, of course), if this is not already done automatically in the current policy. It is in the local investor's best interest to know fairly accurately what the cost of new construction per square foot will be in a particular neighborhood (costs will vary somewhat even within the same city or community). Find out what insurance agents, municipal building authorities, and builders are using as their "rule of thumb" for current new construction costs. Differentiate between the costs for wood frame, masonry, or aggregate block construction. Always compare this "hypothetical construction cost" per square foot with the current *asking* price per square foot of any attractive dwelling on the market.

11. Total Square Footage of the Lot, Dimensions of the Lot, etc.

Lot size is another variable that often cannot be accurately assessed by the potential buyer without ordering or at least seeing the report of an official survey. The degree to which this may be a critical concern will vary with individual circumstances. The potential buyer should always be alert for possible boundary disputes, encroachments by vegetation, masonry, fences, or new construction. The potential buyer should also be wary of possible easements if the property is in the path of any necessary or common access to either public or private property. Typically, a large lot will preserve the true value of an investment property and enhance the resale potential. Overly large lots, however, can be progressively greater burdens for the investor since land cannot be depreciated, too many dollars can be tied up in holding the land, and there will be progressively greater maintenance needs with unusually large lots. Single-family dwellings with X-amount of acreage are probably very inefficient investments except for the owner-occupant. At the other extreme, lots which are abnormally small for the area in which they are located can represent a substantial liability when it comes time to refinance, sell, or exchange the property. Experienced salespersons tend to dismiss the inordinately small lot with pat phrases such as: "Not much yard work with this one!" It is the potential buyer who must critically decide what is acceptable for his/her own purposes with respect to square footage of the building and of the lot on which it is located.

The true dimensions of an income-property lot may be reflected in the recorded legal description. Any complexity or ambiguity in the legal description of the lot or from a visual inspection of the lot may suggest the desirability of looking further for established survey records. In any situation where there needs to be a clarification of the boundaries, or anticipated changes near the boundaries upon change of ownership, it may be worthwhile to require that a legal survey be completed as a condition of the sale. Even in situations where you may be expected to pay for a qualitative legal survey from your own funds, this can be a "wise investment" relative to the time and money that could be absorbed in a potential lawsuit regarding boundary definition and assumed encroachment (see Glossary). Most of the time it will not be necessary to be so cautious and formal about the understood boundaries between adjoining properties. The one other thing that an official survey can provide, however, is a precise definition of that amount of land which is part of the city or county right of way. This can be a critical question when the potential buyer has plans to make significant changes, such as installing a fence or retaining wall in a way that affects the municipal right of way. Curbing, pavement, and sidewalks are also significant factors which involve the municipal right of way. Their absence or presence can alter the value and attractiveness of a particular income-producing property. "Bargain" properties which are located on side streets and lacking both road and sidewalk "improvements" are typically in neighborhoods where you would *never* be able to obtain the written consent of approximately two-thirds of the affected *owners* to have such expensive improvements completed. Test before you buy.

12. County's Assessed Value and Taxes Paid Last Year

It is most important, if not critical, for the investor to verify the amount of property taxes paid during the last year because this is a major determinant of value and will be an unavoidable expense at the moment the investor assumes ownership of the property. In most acquisitions the buyer is obligated to reimburse the seller for the prorated amount of taxes which had already been placed in reserves for the fiscal year. In the case of single-family dwellings, this expense is commonly the largest single "closing cost" in addition to the down payment. You can predict with some assurance that property taxes will continue to increase at a rate somewhat comparable with the actual rate of inflation over the past two to three years (cost of government increases as taxes increase and vice versa). The investor's task is to formally verify the current year's taxes, *before* making an offer to buy, through a search of public records to verify the basis for assessment and the amount of taxes levied in the current and recent years. This procedure will give you an accurate indication of the amount of increase each year over perhaps the last three to five years. Ask yourself if these figures accurately reflect the changes in the valuation of the property. Are the increases steady or abrupt? Has there been a recent increase, or are you likely to be the recipient of a large increase soon after you assume ownership? This latter question is a very real concern in purchasing first-owner buildings in which the assessed tax rate is probably based upon undeveloped land values only and will be assessed at or about the same value as the purchase price soon after you buy it. The builder-seller may be presenting you with an unrealistically low estimate of debt service and other expenses.

The county's assessed valuation in some towns, neighborhoods, or zoning districts may be quite accurate and directly reflect the recent sale price or comparable value at some recent date. In other instances the county may be using a broad formula for different tax districts, and the property you have in mind may be receiving unduly favorable or unfavorable tax treatment. Another instance which is not at all easy to be aware of, or to verify, is that a particular property may have received favorable tax treatment (unrealistically low assessment) due to the connections of the current owner. Radical changes in the assessment might be made soon after you took possession. The income-property investor should get to know the community well enough to anticipate probable tax assessment or zoning changes with some degree of accuracy. This is only one method of ascertaining true market value. There are definitely other, more reliable, methods of determining the approximate market value of most income-producing properties.

13. Financial Terms Desired

The most common expression that buyers of single-family dwellings will hear when inquiring about the type of financial terms desired is: "The seller wants a *cash-out*." Naturally, the seller is looking for that type of buyer who will be able to obtain all of the desired financing *someplace else*—namely, a savings and loan association, bank, a government-insured loan, private party, etc. The sales agent prefers this method of finance to be assured of collecting the agreed-upon commission from the down payment to the seller. This has come to be the "accepted" method of financing owner-occupied, single-family dwellings. From the buyer's point of view, this is the expensive method of purchasing property, especially in a persistently inflationary economy with high sale prices, high interest rates, and tough mortgage conditions. All of this is not so noticeable to the "home" buyer (if they can even obtain the desired loan) when the amount of the required down payment is only 5% to 15% of the total price. The investor (non-owner occupant) is obligated to consider all the expensive considerations of a "conventional" loan and then be required to put down at least 25% to 35% of the total sale price! To avoid the prohibitive limitations of "conventional" financing in a very tight money market, the investor must be prepared to "educate" potential sellers about the *other* means of financing that may be available, legally binding, and capable of being tailored to the seller's and the buyer's needs. The investor can make some good assumptions about the seller's needs by gathering and analyzing data about the seller's current equity, current reason for selling, current age, and probable tax bracket. Seller's "problems" can often be equitably and resourcefully resolved when there is sufficient information about the seller's motivation and financial consequences under different methods of financing. The same careful, yet unobtrusive, method of reasoning can be readily applied to sellers of income-producing properties where the quantity and quality of producible income and the tax consequences for the seller are major decision-making factors. In the recent "seller's market," is was the buyer who had to be the resourceful idea person who did lots of "homework" to tactfully and authoritatively persuade the seller to consider a price, terms, and general methods of financing which were mutually beneficial, not something that was rigidly predetermined by the seller only. The following chapter on conventional and creative ways to finance real estate will elaborate upon the suggested alternatives for conventional financing.

14. Notes

This open-ended section of Investor's Initial Inquiry Form is intended to provide an unstructured place to record intangible feelings, impressions, or other data which may ultimately have some bearing on the decision to abandon the property in question, submit a "ridiculous offer," or seriously attempt to evaluate and negotiate the prospects further in trying to obtain the best, mutually beneficial price and terms for a given income-producing property.

The following is a sample questionnaire which can be utilized in its present form or altered to meet specific needs (if used at all). The intent is to tactfully confront the seller with a series of relevant questions that may or may not be legally binding and which can only be reasonably answered by the current owner. Premature handling of this questionnaire could result in a stalled or lost sale. The most effective means for having this questionnaire completed as requested is to wait until the earnest money agreement has been prepared and then insert the formal request that this questionnaire be completed as a condition of the earnest money agreement. This procedure can help to create a legitimate "out" in an earnest money agreement that is later found by the buyer to be undesirable. *Always* make the earnest money agreement subject to review and approval by your own attorney and/or certified public accountant for the same reason. Reluctance on the part of the seller to complete the requested questionnaire within a reasonable period of time can be a strong indication that the property is not strictly what it has been represented to be. At such a time the buyer and seller could mutually agree to dissolve the earnest money agreement or perhaps have a new basis to re-negotiate the price and other terms of sale.

SELLER'S SUMMARY OF PROPERTY CONDITION AND EXPENSES

Property identification _____ Date_____

1. Anticipated or recent zoning changes	yes	no
2. Anticipated or recent assessment changes (property tax)	yes	no
3. Any special conditions, restrictions, or easements	yes	no
4. Any known building code violations	yes	no
5. Property in compliance with local fire code	yes	no
6. Property free from safety and health hazards	yes	no
7. Property fully insulated and reasonable to heat	yes	no
8. Heating system operational and not in need of repair	yes	no
9. No known termite, pest, dry rot, leaks, or moisture problems	yes	no
10. Any financial concessions to obtain current renters	yes	no

Buying Income-Producing Property 115

11. Any delinquent rent or legal problem with current renters   yes   no
12. Any personal property not included in the sale   yes   no
13. Adequate on- and off-street parking for tenants and visitors   yes   no
14. Adequate on-site laundry facilities for all tenants   yes   no
15. Adequate garbage-disposal facilities for all tenants   yes   no
16. Any current service contracts with community vendors   yes   no
17. Any known problems with plumbing, sewer, or drainage   yes   no
18. Any refusal to provide property with utilities or insurance   yes   no

Summary of Routine Income and Expenses:
A. Total gross income from all sources for the past 12 months _____
B. Total rent per unit for the past 12 months:

Unit	Size	Rent	Unit	Size	Rent	Unit	Size	Rent
1	___	___	9	___	___	17	___	___
2	___	___	10	___	___	18	___	___
3	___	___	11	___	___	19	___	___
4	___	___	12	___	___	20	___	___
5	___	___	13	___	___	21	___	___
6	___	___	14	___	___	22	___	___
7	___	___	15	___	___	23	___	___
8	___	___	16	___	___	24	___	___

C. Total percentage of vacancy for the past 12 months _____
D. Total amount of cleaning and related fees charged for move in _____
E. Total professional management costs for past 12 months _____
F. Total resident manager costs for past 12 months _____
G. Total cost of advertising for past 12 months _____
H. Total cost of garbage collections for past 12 months _____
I. Total cost for water and sewer for past 12 months _____
J. Total cost for electricity for past 12 months _____
K. Total cost for heat for the past 12 months _____
L. Total cost for housekeeping services for past 12 months _____
M. Total cost for maintenance and repairs for past 12 months _____

116 Real Estate Investment

N. Total cost of cleaning and painting for past 12 months _____
O. Total cost of grounds maintenance for past 12 months _____
P. Total cost of all insurance for past 12 months _____
Q. Total cost of all property taxes for past taxable year _____

Seller's signature_____Date_____
Witnessed by _____Date_____

7

Conventional and Creative Methods of Financing Real Estate

Four Basic Forms of Financing
1. Conventional
2. Federal
3. State
4. Private

CONVENTIONAL FINANCING

This is the most common and most familiar type of financing. Any time that you receive a loan from a bank, savings and loan, credit union, commercial bank, mutual savings bank, or a loan company, you have probably obtained a "conventional" loan—that is, any loan which is secured by a definable asset (in real estate, usually a mortgage, trust deed, or subordinate mortgage) and a fixed percentage of down payment (typically 20%-10%-5% down for owner-occupied dwellings and 30%-25%-20% down for commercial, or "investment," property) *and* the current market interest rate—this is a *conventional* loan. Refinancing an existing property (acquiring a subordinate mortgage in second or third position) is also generally a form of conventional financing. The only thing that is "conventional" about the loans described above is that the lender is in the position to prescribe *all* of the terms and conditions of the loan, including prepayment penalties, term of the loan, appraisals, surveys, loan application fees, mortgage insurance, etc.

FEDERAL FINANCING

This is the second most familiar type of financing for most individuals. The two most familiar sources—V.A. and F.H.A.—are not literally sources of funding. Veterans Administration loans and Federal Housing Authority loans are actually insurance policies which back conventional lenders up to 100% of the approved loan. In general terms, F.H.A. and V.A. are legislatively approved insurance programs to assist veterans and non-veterans who are essentially "first-time" buyers to acquire an owner-occupied residence with little or no money down. The "eligibility" for these "insurance programs" is quite loosely defined with regards to single-family, owner-occupant dwellings within a price range up to approximately $60,000. One of the few limitations is that the same individual or same family cannot utilize either of these programs more often than once every two calendar years. The intent of the program was to make private ownership of a residential dwelling financially accessible to large numbers of families and some individuals who would reside in them for two years *or longer*. Non-resident "investors" are discouraged by requiring that all of the basic standards be applied *plus* an additional down payment of at least 15% to make the transaction equivalent to ordinary conventional financing. There are lower income standards applied for eligibility, but no upper income limitations. Despite the credit standing of the borrower, conventional lenders (non-thrift institutions) are typically not interested in V.A. or F.H.A. insurance on residential mortgage loans because of the customary 30-to-35 year terms *and* the obligation to accept the current interest rate proposed by either the V.A. or F.H.A. To compensate the conventional lender, the federal government allows them to charge a one-time-only number of "discount points," which are basically the percentage points of difference between the currently defined V.A. or F.H.A. interest rate and the yield that major mortgage buyers can obtain through the current market interest rate charged by the conventional lender. In times of extremely high interest rates, V.A. and F.H.A.-

insured loans can be attractive to borrowers and most unattractive to lenders. The fee for obtaining an F.H.A.-insured loan is ¼ of 1% per month. One of the subtle distinctions between the two is that V.A. mortgages are guaranteed rather than insured. Therefore, there are no insurance premiums to be paid. Another distinction is that V.A. mortgages are available only to qualified veterans and military personnel, and in some cases their spouses may be eligible.

In the past decade, F.H.A. in particular has suffered immensely from its inability to rapidly adjust to perpetual inflation, rapidly changing interest rates, and frequent scandal. F.H.A. Section 221 D.2, the familiar minimum down payment program, almost became extinct until the ceiling was raised to approximately $60,000. Section 220 authorizes the insurance of loans connected with the rehabilitation of low-income housing and new construction to replace slum dwellings. Sections 213 and 236 authorize the insurance of mortgages on cooperative housing projects. Section 235 is now considered defunct due to repeated embarrassment that was brought on by the manipulation of Section 235 construction guidelines and the sale of 235 homes to "unqualified" buyers who soon went into default so the process could be repeated over and over again.

The federal government sponsors insurance on real estate loans and/or direct government loans in approximately 40 to 50 different programs. Many of these variations are within F.H.A. and V.A., including the F.H.A. and V.A. farm-loan insurance programs. There are potential S.B.A. loans (insurance again), special minority grants and loans, and a wide range of programs administrered by the Department of Housing and Urban Development (HUD). The Housing Division's Multi-Unit Housing Financing Program for designated populations is merely one of these.

STATE FINANCING

The Department of Housing and Urban Development has its counterpart in each of the fifty states. These state housing authorities have their own source of funds to lend for substantial rehabilitation projects and construction of multi-unit housing for designated populations—elderly, low-income, and handicapped (and in that approximate order, or combinations thereof). The "red tape" in working directly with a large governmental body and of seeing to the best interests of Section 8, subsidy tenants, can be profound. The rewards can also be great for the right individual or group of individual investors.

The least familiar source of financing for most persons is probably the local state G.I. loan. The obvious reason for the lack of familiarity is that eligibility is restricted to certain veterans who are residents of the particular state. The veterans must then demonstrate their ability to maintain the mortgage payments, and find an acceptable residential property in which the seller will consider meeting the standards for state G.I. approval. This has become an increasingly rare phenomenon as residential dwelling prices increase from 10% to 30% per year! Also, the state G.I. loan can typically be obtained only one time during the lifetime of a particular veteran. The eligible state G.I. must be prepared to "settle down" in a particular place and at a particular time. The other restriction is that the loan must be used for an approved owner-occupant dwelling only. The incentive for all this effort can be the 5.6% loan up to approximately $45,000. Conventional loan monies will probably never reach such a low level again. A final advantage of state G.I. financing is that anyone can assume the loan balance at 5.6% if they are eligible veterans, and non-veterans can assume the loan at 7.0%. This favorable interest rate can be used to create many interesting options for an investor.

Private Financing

The term "private financing" will be used here to refer to the buying and selling of income-producing property on a contract (land sales contract, installment contract, land contract, trust deed contract, and related terms). It is through the medium of legally binding "contracts" that investment properties can be transferred from one investor to another without the uncompromising, overly conservative and expensive "conventional" loans. In most communities throughout the nation, apartment complexes in particular are transferred from one party to another almost exclusively by contract. To get a favorable price, the seller must often yield more than the "conventional money market" would allow. The conventional wisdom of being "cashed out" as a result of a newly created 70% loan can actually be *unattractive* to a prospective seller. The tax law is such that in receiving over 29% of the total saleprice, the seller can be obligated to pay a most unattractive amount of capital gains tax for the year of sale.

One solution is to create a legally binding contract which in turn creates an *installment sale*. The full impact of the capital gains taxes can now be deferred over a prescribed number of years that could be much more individually suited to the needs of, and the tax bracket of, the seller.

Another solution to a specific set of needs could be to create a legally binding contract for the *exchange* of investment properties between two or more parties and create a 100% capital gains tax deferral for each party "trading up" and an ordinary capital gains tax event for each party "trading down." The possibilities for mutual agreement within a secure, legally binding contract can be virtually unlimited. Each property is different, and the particular needs of each investor is different. A properly prepared contract always permits more give and take in each potential element of a financial transaction than the standardized, ritualized, and one-sided conventional loan.

In periods of tight money, persistent inflation, and high fluctuating interest rates, conventional lenders often "don't have the money to lend!" The thrift institutions are under great pressure, as are the national banks, to sell newly required mortgages and therefore "buy" large quantities of money from the "Fed" and centralized banks and institutional sources. They are losing most of their inexpensive monies as depositors flee from accounts paying 5¼% to 8½% to federal, private, and corporate sources paying from 9¼% to 13% on relatively short-term time deposits. The thrift institutions, credit unions and national banks must pay a prime rate of from 9% to 15% themselves! Long-term mortgage loans would potentially have to be offered at a net loss! Instead, many institutional lenders are restricting themselves to short-term "consumer loans" and industrial loans which are only a very few percentage points above their cost to obtain large sums of money. Such periods of economic crisis limit the number of "conventional buyers" as well and help to make the land sales contract a more attractive proposal for the seller who has a genuine desire to sell and the resourceful buyer who can favorably adjust the terms to accommodate the reality of inflated sale prices.

BUYING AND SELLING ON CONTRACT

The "contract" (land sales contract, land contract, purchase money mortgage, trust deed contract,* and related terms) is a common instrument in the financing of investment properties. A contract, by whatever name, is essentially a legally binding document which is created between two or more parties, and with the assistance of a knowledgeable attorney, to assure compliance in a defined financial agreement between buyer and seller and secured by a mortgage for a portion of the purchase price. The basic elements of any valid, legally binding contract are as follows:

1. Any contract for the sale or exchange of real property must be in *writing* (and usually made up by an attorney with a knowledgeable background in real estate contracts).
2. A *lawful proposal* must be *communicated* by one party and

---

*Avoid the trust deed contract if you do not own the property free and clear and if you are merely trying to shorten the period of foreclosure. A better method is to utilize a land sales contract with an *executed* quit claim deed in escrow with your personal attorney. The quit claim deed can be recorded in the event of a formally defined default.

freely accepted by the other (both must be of lawful age and mentally competent).
3. The *acceptance* must be communicated to the offeror and it must be unqualified. Any counter-offer is legally considered to be a rejection of the most recent offer, and the process must either be revised or abandoned.
4. A contract must be *definitive* and *non-ambiguous* to be enforceable. The language of the contract must clearly define the *mutual intent* of all directly accountable parties.
5. All contracts must be supported by *consideration*—i.e., the defined agreement to exchange something of value (usually expressed in terms of dollars) for either an equity interest or titled interest in the defined real property.
6. There must be *acknowledgment* in the form of written signatures by all defined parties & usually witnessed by a notary public.
7. The contract must be promptly *recorded* "for all the world to see" and in the appropriate county of the real property.

The rationale for the extensive use of the "contract" in the acquisition and sale of real property has been a matter of necessity. Conventional, bank-style financing has often been too expensive, too conservative, and not always available (especially to investors!). This dilemma is consistently true in a rapidly inflating economy with double-digit interest rates and precariously high prices for acquisition, monthly installments, upgrading, and general maintenance of real property. The odds are that there will be a distinct difference between the cash available and the amount required for the down payment. The absence of additional financing to erase the difference between the seller's required down payment and the buyer's available cash would cause most transactions with investment properties to fail. The common solution in filling this financial gap is to obtain secondary financing from a commercial lender (rarely approved because of the "weak equity" position, and then only at rates "commensurate" with the lender's demands) *or* by obtaining the seller's interest in accepting a contract for the balance of the down payment, a possible "wrap-around mortgage," and related. The motivation of the seller is that a favorable price can be obtained and an installment sale can be created to reduce the burden of the capital gains tax to be paid. Under such circumstances it is quite likely that such a seller will accept secondary financing at interest rates which are below the prevailing market. A third incentive for the seller is the basic control of the terms of the contract, especially the minimum amount to be paid monthly and the *term* of the contract. A 4-to-5-year equity payoff is tending to be much more common. A particularly stubborn seller might be able to reduce the term to approximately 3 years, or less!

ADVANTAGES FOR THE CONTRACT BUYER

1. Acquisition and control of an otherwise prohibitive investment
2. Substantial benefits to be derived from the use of leverage
3. Variability in negotiating the interest rate to be charged
4. Absence of conventional fees such as the 1% to 2% loan application fee, pre-payment penalties, acceleration clauses, appraisal fees, survey fee, highest current market interest rates, loan insurance, credit reports, etc.
5. Flexibility in mutually agreeing upon all terms and conditions
6. An equity interest in real property which is readily assignable to another party, refinancable, and a source of income production
7. Secondary financing irregardless of the availability of funds through conventional sources

THE DIRECT APPROACH

A brief letter can be addressed to a prospective seller (approach owners before they get locked into media saturation and/or agency listings) which introduces you, your request to purchase their income-producing property, and the basic potential advantages to seller and buyer. A sample of such a letter could be as follows:

March 1, 1980

Mr. & Mrs. George D. Sellers
1200 N. Michigan Ave.
Chicago, Illinois 60611

Dear Mr. and Mrs. Sellers,

I would like to respectfully submit an offer to purchase the four-plex located at 2724 N. Park Ave., Chicago, Illinois.

The intent of this letter is to inquire about the potential to submit an offer o purchase a specific property from one private party to another. In absoluately no way are any parties or interests involved in this offer other than myself. Everything stated in this letter is fully subject to verification.

I would like to purchase the above-mentioned property directly from you on a land sales contract. I would appreciate the opportunity to at least briefly discuss this offer at your earliest convenience. With your consent I would be quite willing to have a draft legal contract prepared for the sale of the above property. This contract could then be reviewed in detail by your own attorney and/or tax advisor to be absolutely confident that your own interests are met and well protected.

Advantages for the Seller:

1. A current fair-market price for the above indicated property should distinctly enhance the overall return on the original investment.
2. The creation of a well-structured *installment sale* can reduce the amount of capital gains tax to be paid to the absolute minimum. Future tax shelter may erase most or all of the capital gains tax.
3. The cost of sale (preparations, advertising, commissions, and related costs) will be virtually non-existent.
4. The terms and conditions of the sale can be precisely and individually suited to both seller and buyer. There can be much flexibility in mutually agreeing to terms and conditions such as the price, interest rate, minimum monthly payment, date of equity payoff, and other seller controls.
5. The seller's current titled interest or equity interest in the above property will remain intact, and a full repossession could occur in

the case of a formally defined default in the receipt of the monthly payments.
6. An equity payoff at the end of 36 months would be acceptable.

Advantages for the Buyer:

1. Acquisition of a fairly priced income-producing property
2. Acquisition of a new "basis" for purposes of depreciation
3. Flexibility in mutually agreeing to terms and conditions, such as the price, interest rate, minimum monthly payments, date of equity payoff and related buyer concerns
4. Avoidance of conventional financing which can be arbitrary, capricious, and overly expensive regarding "investment" properties in terms of money shortages, high percentage of down payment, pre-payment penalties, acceleration clauses, loan application fees, appraisal fees, survey fees, other inspections, mortgage (not title) insurance, maximum possible interest rates, and related
5. An initial down payment and first-year principle payment of *less* than 30%
6. Agreement to pay off any equity balance within an unusually short period of time through refinance, resale, or other means, in exchange for the favorable terms and conditions indicated above

I would be most anxious to discuss this request with you at the earliest possible time. I can generally be reached on the weekends or evenings at 824-7003.

Thank you for your consideration.

Most Sincerely,

Jay M. Kimmel

VALUE OF A CONTRACT FROM THE SELLER'S POINT OF VIEW

1. The annual interest rate to be received can be firmly negotiated (up or down) without being bound by the current commercial and institutional lenders' rate of interest.

2. The interest rate and the many terms and conditions can

be carefully written to be commensurate with the perceived level of risk. Secondary financing will obviously have a higher rate of interest and more definitive terms than a contract which is secured by a first mortgage.

3. A contract can be formally structured to create and guarantee an installment sale. This method (rule of 30%) is similar to income averaging and allows the seller to spread out the capital gains tax to be paid on the computed proceeds of sale.

4. The seller can often obtain a more favorable sale price and build in more flexible terms to suit both the seller and buyer by being willing to accept a contract.

5. A well-secured contract with acceptable (to the seller) interest rates and minimum monthly payments (assured by formal penalties) can be an end result in itself. This is especially true when a seller is retired or anticipates retirement in the near future and wants "passive" income which will not interfere with social security income, pension plans, etc.

6. A land contract or mortgage paper can be sold on the "mortgage paper" market. However, there are at least two potential problems in doing this that can have severe consequences. First, a discount in the face value of the contract is almost certain. Secondly, sale of the contract triggers the tax event for that year. The consequences of either outcome should be carefully evaluated by your accountant before entering into the transaction.

7. Investors in mortgage paper (like investors in bonds) are concerned about *yield*. The investor who buys a $100,000 note at 10% annual interest for 5 years must pay income tax on the interest received. The return is considered to be sub-standard to unacceptable *unless* the $100,000 note is already discounted and will be cashed out at, say, $125,000 at the end of the 5 years. Now the yield is $5,000 per year plus the interest after taxes.

8. With some degree of creativity and a well-structured and typically "seasoned" contract, there is potential to use that contract as collateral or as part of a new down payment with little or no discount. The use of a contract as collateral against a new loan

should be relatively self-explanatory. The possible tax trap that can occur under these circumstances is when the contract is used at 100% of face value, the I.R.S. reviewers may interpret that as a conversion in that year rather than the eventual payout date and therefore trigger a totally unexpected tax event!

9. An "attractive" contract equity can be converted to an income-property equity by using that contract as near-face-value collateral for the payment of a note which has been created for the balance of the purchase price on an income property of your choice.

10. Another common method of converting contract equities to near face value would be as follows: Mr. Athercrombie sells an income-producing property for $100,000. He receives $20,000 as a cash down payment. He accepts a land sales contract for the balance of $80,000. The contract specifies that he is to receive payments of no less than $1,000 per month, and the equity balance is to be due at the end of the fifth year (installment sale). One year later Mr. Athercrombie purchases a much larger income-producing property as follows:

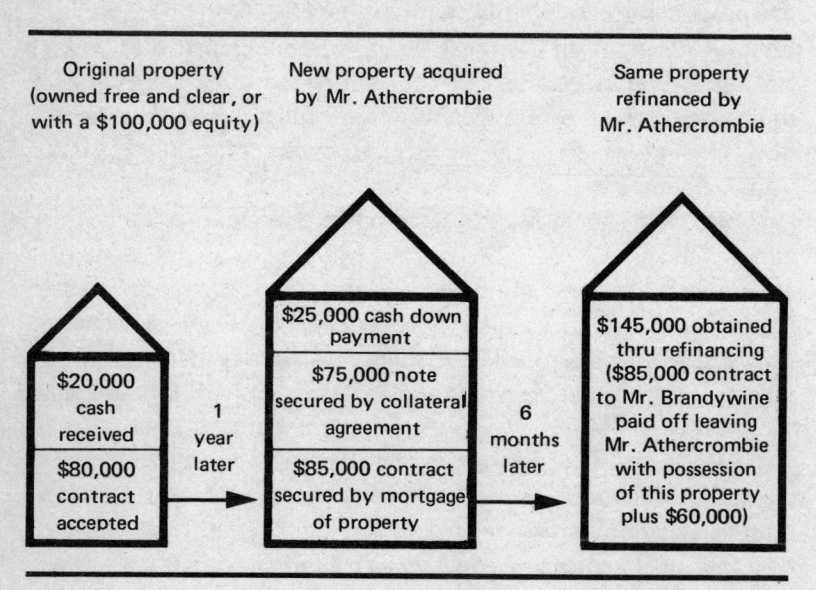

Original property (owned free and clear, or with a $100,000 equity)	New property acquired by Mr. Athercrombie	Same property refinanced by Mr. Athercrombie
$20,000 cash received	$25,000 cash down payment	$145,000 obtained thru refinancing ($85,000 contract to Mr. Brandywine paid off leaving Mr. Athercrombie with possession of this property plus $60,000)
$80,000 contract accepted	$75,000 note secured by collateral agreement	
	$85,000 contract secured by mortgage of property	

(1 year later → 6 months later)

Price: $185,000 with a down payment of $25,000. The remaining balance of $160,000 was "creatively financed." The new seller, Mr. Brandywine, accepted a land sales contract in the amount of $85,000 which was secured by the mortgage on the $185,000 property. He also accepted a $75,000 note which was secured by a collateral agreement using the contract which had been created by the original sale.

The result of this second transaction is that Mr. Athercrombie now has a $100,000 equity in the newly acquired income property. He was able to accomplish this goal by effectively converting his land sales contract to an income-property equity at near face value. This process could easily be carried another step further if Mr. Athercrombie were to refinance this second property for $145,000. Since there are no taxes on borrowed money, Mr. Athercrombie can now pay off Mr. Brandywine (approximately $85,000) and have an additional $60,000 to pursue an entirely new investment. The possible variations on the above methods are virtually endless. All use the same basic principles of creative financing. A schematic illustration would be as follows:

The conversion of equities (contractual or real property) can be structured to occur almost simultaneously and involve many different parties with different resources and desires. The motivation in most instances is to exercise a maximum amount of leverage by creating a tax-deferred situation in all upward exchanges. Variety is enhanced as various parties enter into a "multiple exchange" in which a certain chain of events is accepted subject to a potentially large number of definable events occurring at the time of closing. The owner of a free-and-clear house, for instance, might exchange that equity for possession of a larger, income-producing property, *on the condition* that the free-and-clear house is *pre-sold* to a third party at the time of closing. A classic reference on this particular topic is Richard R. Reno's *Profitable Real Estate Exchanging and Counseling*, which was published by Prentice-Hall, Inc., Englewood Cliffs, N.J., 1965.

DEVELOPING AND FINANCING A LARGE APARTMENT COMPLEX

1. The first step is to develop plans and specifications.
2. The second step is to prepare a "feasibility study" (the amount to be financed will depend on economics, not cost).
   a. This study must demonstrate how much income the property will produce.
   b. Demonstrate that there *is* a market for this service at the price necessary to be self-sufficient—*e.g.*, rent of 40¢ per foot times 800 square feet will produce $320 per month. How realistic is this rental rate? What will the demand be? Will there be any rent subsidy paid by secondary sources?
   c. Determine the costs to build the project, cost of land, taxes, maintenance, expenses, management, and related.
   d. Determine the net income (rule of thumb: estimate 38% of gross income for all expenses prior to interest and amortization).
   e. Take these criteria to an appropriate builder (one that you have personally selected and researched to meet your own standards) and request that the builder modify your design to fit the figures. A good engineer-builder and/or architectural engineer knows how much things are going to cost. If the design cannot be modified to fit the figures, it is *unfeasible!*
3. Now that you have successfully completed the feasibility study, the third step is to explore and obtain the approval for the financing *before* making any commitments (and/or options) to purchase the building site. Allow approximately 10% to 15% of the total cost for the land. Successful completion of the project could entail the following financial instruments: a land loan, building loan, permanent financing, note payable to the general contractor, and a note payable to the broker, if any.
   a. *Never* sign a contract with a builder or general contractor

until financing is absolutely assured in writing and from dependable sources. *Insist* that a penalty clause be inserted in the contract to build which states exactly how much the builder must pay the developer for each day beyond the agreed-upon deadline *and* that the builder is liable for financial penalties that may be imposed by the lender for failure to meet the construction deadline.

b. In times of unusually tight money supplies, seriously explore the private and less commonly sought-after sources of financing. The following is a list of potential money sources other than national banks:

Charitable Institutions	Mortgage Investment Companies
College, University Trusts	Mutual Savings Banks
Commercial Banks	Pension Funds
Corporate Trust Funds	Private Individuals, Partnerships
Estate Executors	R.E.I.T.'s (Mortgage Trusts)
Foundations	Savings and Loan Associations
Fraternal Orders	Seller (Contract, Purchase Money Mortgage)
	State and Federal Government

c. Use your imagination to creatively augment your percentage of down payment (beware of the risks of "over-financing" and concealment of your true indebtedness) and directly apply at conventional sources such as local savings and loan associations, mutual savings banks, and related. Be sensitive to the advice and suggestions that they may offer. Many times they have had experience with similar loans in your particular community. With effort you might be able to meet their tough, ultra-conservative standards.

d. Consider legally defined limited partnerships and related (syndication, co-operatives, incorporation) to increase your financial base.

Consider meeting the profusion of guidelines to obtain government financing by making application under one of their various "priority programs."
f. Consider second and third mortgage loans with interest rates that are above the current market and for relatively short terms. Also consider possible subordination with the seller of the land, or the builder, etc. Be resourceful. Be devious, if necessary, but never dishonest.

VARIATIONS ON THE "NO-MONEY-DOWN" THEME

Locate a seller whose income needs and tax situation are suitable so that he or she would be willing to enter into a binding agreement to sell you a particular property and at a designated price *after* the seller *refinances* the high-equity property to obtain the desired amount of money (tax free!). Example: seller agrees to sell an older duplex for $50,000. The sale-price equity is $30,000. The seller agrees to refinance the existing $20,000 balance up to $35,000. This new loan gives the seller $15,000 of tax-free money (no tax on borrowed money) and a much lower-taxed installment sale with a contract on the original $50,000 payable at 1.25% per month. The buyer acquires a $50,000 asset with tremendous tax shelter benefits (distinct negative cash flow) for the price of minor closing costs only!

The example given above applies especially well in situations where the seller has a free and clear ownership of the desired property. The potential for creative refinancing is almost unlimited as long as the funds are available. In carefully controlled situations (a fully binding legal contract), the sellers may be induced to raise their sale price by, say, $5,000 and take back a second note against the original property. This can give the buyer full control of the original property with almost no money down *and* an additional $5,000 in cash to go out and buy more real estate!

The Veterans Administration routinely offers 100% financing to eligible persons who are seeking owner-occupied residences up to approximately four units. This can be an ideal opportunity for an eligible person to fully utilize the principle of leverage and within a reasonable time convert the single or multiple units entirely into income-producing units. The formal rules and guidelines suggested by the V.A. must be rigorously followed to avoid future complications. F.H.A. loans can approximate 100% financing, and, like the V.A., have been a starting point for millions of persons who might otherwise spend years "saving up" for that inflationary down payment.

Creative "over-financing" can be achieved in the conventional loan market if the borrower has a benefactor (such as a parent) who will make a non-recorded loan to the potential conventional borrower to satisfy the requirements of a typical savings and loan institution for an owner-occupied residential dwelling. In effect, this is equivalent to 100% financing. The borrower treats the family's extension of funds as their own money rather than as a "loan." The risk that is taken in such situations is that the borrower may suddenly be unable to keep up with the "double" mortgage payment and seriously jeopardize the true nature of the original unofficial loan. The parents' money might be lost only if they were also unable to continue the monthly mortgage payments. In short-term arrangements in which there is upgrading and a profitable sale, the unofficial loan can often be erased.

Other methods of financing income-producing properties without commitment of your own funds tend to be variations of the above suggestions, or an entirely different class of creative financing in which the emphasis is upon rapid transfer or conversion of funds from "pre-sold" units to cover all costs from land acquisition to the final sale, refinance, or exchange of a completed income property. The details of such transactions are considered to be essentially beyond the scope of this particular text. It is through the creative application of the three basic means of real estate finance (sale, refinance, or exchange) that all income-producing properties are acquired, "pyramided," or disposed of. One of the methods that is a little different would be as follows:

ACQUIRE A $100,000 ASSET WITH NO MONEY DOWN

The approximate variables necessary to create a legally sound real estate investment of $100,000 (or any other amount) with no money down could be set up in the following manner:

1. Locate a seller who is retired or near retirement age and who wants to sell a free and clear, low-basis property (farm land, etc.) at an acceptable price—*e.g.*, $100,000—without paying the prohibitive capital gains taxes that would result from a cash sale.

2. In exchange for the deed to the property, the buyer gives the seller a contract with an agreeable monthly payment for the natural life of the seller! This can be "statistically" determined by the actuarial curves of any major life insurance company. If the seller were to die within a short period of time, the buyer would have a free and clear deed with no further payments. Of course, if the seller lives to be 99, the long-term consequences could be expensive.

3. The problem that enters into this arrangement is that the *buyer* could die long before the seller could get his or her price out of the sale. The solution to the problem is for the buyer to take out life insurance which is equal in value to the total price of the sale and name the seller as the sole beneficiary. The interests of both parties are now well protected. The seller has a virtually tax-free income for life, or a tax-free life insurance payoff if the buyer dies unexpectedly. The local insurance agent gets the benefit of a policy sale. The buyer is free to convert the property for a different use and/or massively refinance the free-and-clear deed to create funds for other investments. All with no money down!

HIGH-PERCENTAGE DOWN PAYMENTS

High-percentage down payments (35% to 50% and more) are typically unpopular with novice investors because of the diminished benefits of financial leverage and the real potential that "too much" cash flow can create, rather than resolve, adjusted income tax problems. Actually, the potential for creative financing can often be better under these circumstances than in any other way! The "creativity" of high-percentage down payments is a direct result of being able to solve a problem that sellers routinely create for themselves. The sellers' common dilemma is that one of the *real* reasons for selling is that they want to raise a large amount of cash. The seller of investment properties is typically planning ahead for the next investment. In the process, the investor tends to become mentally committed to the idea of using the *total* sale-price equity to make some new, highly leveraged investment which will more rapidly increase his/her overall "total yield." One solution for the "seller's bind" (perhaps a premature commitment on another property) is for the seller to accept the "slightly lower" offer which assures the seller of the highest possible percentage of down payment. Surprisingly, *most* buyers will accept the high-percentage down payment in lieu of a smaller down payment and "contract back." The only likely exception in which a big down payment will *not* be attractive is to the seller who is intent upon temporarily deferring all capital gains taxes (exchange upward), or to spread out the obligatory capital gains taxes (installment sale).

As a general rule, few sellers will deviate from their original intentions about the method in which they expect to dispose of an investment property. The buyer can be wasting valuable time in trying to persuade someone to consider a *low*-percentage down payment and an installment sale when the seller is intent upon a high percentage of cash only, or perhaps a trade upward only.

Another distinct advantage of the high-percentage down payment is the ability to attract the interest of virtually all sellers of attractive, well-located, well-managed, and well-maintained properties in the community. It is not necessary to find the "distressed property with the right things wrong," or the undesirable, hidden-value property that will require substantial upgrading. Instead, the "strong buyer" can move exceptionally quickly to consummate an assured sale at a time when speed of closure may be of real importance to the seller. The high-percentage buyer can successfully acquire the most desirable investment properties in the community—the ones that will appreciate most rapidly, stay occupied, and sell at the best prices despite economic fluctuations.

The investor with a limited amount of cash might consider trimming down his or her expectations and at least consider properties which are appropriately priced at approximately two to three times the total amount of cash available. The individual with $25,000 in cash to invest can buy virtually *any* $50,000 to $75,000 property on the market and complete the transaction at a good price and in record time. If desired, the property can now be refinanced for other possible investments and resold at a desirable price after a reasonable period as an income property. The potential variations are relatively unlimited.

8

Tenant Selection For Maximum Profit and Minimum Headache

STARTING OFF RIGHT

Let's assume that you have just acquired a new income-producing property. With careful management and a good rental history, the property will be at least self-sufficient. You can reasonably assume for yourself that careful and appropriate tenant selection will be a very significant factor in the amount of success and satisfaction that will be experienced with this particular property. On this eventful "first day of possession" of that multiple-unit complex, you will become acutely aware of the fact that you have just "inherited" a flock of tenants that you did not select, that you know very little about, and who know even less about you! Be prepared. You're suddenly going to hear about problems that you never imagined would exist: unfulfilled "promises" by the previous owner, maintenance problems requiring *immediate* attention, and complaints about "other" tenants. Suddenly you may be locked into a tough adversary relationship in re-establishing an owner/manager-versus-tenant "position" (*cf.* pecking order) with both the aggressive and the passive-aggressive tenants. Are you going to be an authoritarian *gorilla* shouting rules from the parking lot, or a meek *ostrich* with an inability to make or consistently enforce minimum basic rules? The stress that the inherited tenant may be experiencing

138 Real Estate Investment

can be described psychologically as a desire for reassurance that their basic housing needs and expectations will be met. As a result of the stress, there will be numerous probes to quickly test the reactions of the new owner/manager. The early impressions and reactions of the new owner/manager will determine much about the behavior of many tenants who may go to extremes to test the limits and/or take advantage of the new situation. The owner/manager in this "first-day" situation will do well to attentively take notes without making decisions "on the spot," but to quickly and efficiently resolve as many of the reasonable requests as possible and simply ignore the unreasonable requests. If this tactic results in some tenants moving on, all the better. Now you can, in reality, begin your selection process.

AVOID THE BIG MISTAKES

Anticipate the adversary relationship that tends to accompany "inherited" tenants and the similar adversary relationship that tends to develop over time between owner/managers and tenants. Don't over-react to the apparent hostility that the tenant in this relationship may express (directly or passively). Be firm, consistent, and attentive to all tenants and show the respect for them as people that you would show anyone who was willing to make you wealthier by helping to pay off your indebtedness! Keep in mind the changing relationship that occurs between the lender and the borrower. The borrower (*e.g.*, applying at a small-loan office) is usually willing to agree to almost anything and to pour out intimate information about himself or herself to obtain a desired loan. The borrower's goal is to obtain the desired object. Once the desired object is attained, the borrower is left with the residual obligation of making monthly payments which limit the amount of available money in the present. The first few payments were likely made without much reluctance because of the greater satisfaction of obtaining the desired goal. The continuous obligation to make payments soon erodes any positive feelings about making the payments, and the lender is progressively seen in the adversary role of "loan shark," "capitalist money manipulator," "economic parasite," etc. The resentment about making the monthly payments steadily builds. The relationship can become most brittle when there is an economic crisis which further restricts the ability of the borrower to make those monthly payments. A parallel relationship tends to exist and/or develop between owner/managers and tenants. Seemingly small events can trigger very strong responses on either side. The owner/manager must avoid the big mistakes of improperly or illegally responding to a tenant despite possible provocation. In addition to anticipation and temperament, the owner/manager must be very familiar with the basic landlord-tenant laws which may exist in your particular area. Avoid being overly confrontative. Utilize strictly legal remedies. Know exactly how to evict a tenant without precipitating a "battle" or "rent strike," etc. Negotiate when appropriate, but never bluff when you do not fully intend to carry out the bluff when necessary. Be fair. Try to stay out of court.

MINIMIZE PROSPECTS WHO "WANT TO LOOK AROUND"

Newer apartment construction throughout the country is basically so standardized that the amenities from one unit to another are essentially the same. Good location, physical attractiveness, and convenient parking are the three major characteristics that will differentiate one apartment complex from another. When all other things are equal, prospective tenants will shop for the best price if there is some surplus of rental units. These are the time-consuming "be-backs" who "want to look around" a little more and who almost never come back. To reverse this futile activity, you must analyze the positive characteristics of your particular apartment complex and have this information printed in a bound and attractive one- or two-page brochure (a *heavy* plastic binder keeps the prospects from walking away with the brochure and gives the owner or the manager the right to ask for it back). In the brochure you must concisely outline all of the positive features of the apartment complex. Emphasize location (*e.g.*, to major grocery stores, shopping centers, recreation centers, houses of worship, schools, parks, the downtown area, freeway or turnpike access, major employers, restaurants, etc.) because new prospects are often disoriented and ill at ease in a "new territory." Emphasize basic features (*e.g.*, spacious rooms, wall-to-wall carpeting, new, colored appliances, especially dishwashers, garbage disposal, or air-conditioning, new draperies, balconies, view, quietness, storage areas, secure locks, laundry facilities, recreation facilities, visitor parking areas, smoke alarms, or special amenities such as swag lamps, fireplaces, framed pictures, shower or sauna stalls, antenna hook-ups, skylights, etc.) to give the impression that there is greater attention given to detail at this apartment complex than at the one down the road. Emphasize landscaping (physical attractiveness of the exterior of the building or buildings and surrounding grounds is very important to the image that a responsible tenant wants to project to friends and family who will be making visits; also, a well-cared-for and "maintenance-free" living area can be an aesthetic value in itself to capitalize on that important first impression of the rental property to offset the possible frustrations involved in finding a new location for the first time.

THE REQUIRED WRITTEN APPLICATION

Never offer to rent property without obtaining a detailed, written application first. Such recklessness could make you vulnerable to the "professional deadbeats" who set out to create collection-loss problems for the unwary, or even possible housing discrimination suits. A properly prepared application for rental will not screen out all errors in tenant selection. A verified written application *will* immensely improve the percentage for identifying a desirable tenant. The written application is a test of the seriousness of the prospective tenant's desire to actually rent a particular unit, and indirectly it is a reflection of the tenant's desire to adhere to the basic rules and guidelines that are necessary to preserve tranquility among families and individuals who are living in such close proximity to each other. The written application for rental is about the only method for selection of tenants which is not likely to result in a premature acceptance, a confrontation, or a civil suit claiming discrimination on the basis of race, religion, age, sex, marital status, physical handicap, or other single-factor variable. Selection guidelines must be based upon formal criteria which are legally acceptable and have nothing to do with the types of discrimination cited above. It is a natural sequence of events to request that an individual or couple (married or not) complete a rental application once they have indicated an interest in renting the property in question. It is now possible for the owner/manager to remain strictly in control by informing the prospective tenant that applications are being accepted for approximately two days and a decision will be made at the end of that time. If pressed for an earlier decision, the owner/manager can explain that references must be verified first and a decision will be made strictly on the basis of credit references and personal references. Consistency in applying screening criteria is the key to avoiding actionable discrimination charges. The following is a very basic application for rental which may be reproduced as it is or modified to meet individual needs:

APPLICATION FOR RENTAL

Property to be rented _____ Apt._____ Date Wanted_____

Monthly rent_____ Cleaning Fee_____ Damage fee_____ Pet fee_____

Name_____ Soc. Sec. No._____

Present address _____ How long?_____ Phone_____

Landlord's name _____ Phone_____ O.K. to call?_____

Former address_____ How long?_____ Reason moved_____

EMPLOYMENT

Present employer_____ Address_____

Type of work done _____ How long?_____ Present salary_____

Previous employer _____ How long?_____ Former salary_____

Other source of income_____

CREDIT REFERENCES

Please list local credit accounts, VISA, Master Charge, or related references:

1. _____

2. _____

3. _____

4. _____

5. _____

Name of bank_____ Branch_____ Checking_____ Saving_____

Description of car(s)_____

Car financed by_____ Insured by _____

MISCELLANEOUS

Personal reference _____ Phone_____

Personal reference _____ Phone_____

In case of emergency notify _____ Phone_____

Names and ages of children_____ Pets_____

AGREEMENT

The above information has been given to determine current credit status for the purpose of renting the above-mentioned property. It is understood that a written rental agreement will be completed prior to occupancy. This application is subject to approval by the owner and/or his/her officially delegated agent. It is further understood that the law requires 30 days' advance notice in writing of the intention to vacate the above premises. I also acknowledge that the references given above may be formally verified with the local credit bureau.

_____ _____
          Signature   Date

FOUR MOST IMPORTANT CRITERIA FOR TENANT SELECTION

1. Verification of Financial References
2. Verification of Employment and/or Stated Income
3. Verification of Former Rental History
4. Verification of Personal References

VERIFICATION OF FINANCIAL REFERENCES

Each of the above criteria must be verified to your own personal satisfaction. It is generally not enough to accept references on their stated "face value" alone. An unverified application will be of little value after the fact when a currently delinquent tenant is found to have been troublesome and delinquent with the former landlord, or someone who consistently failed to make payments on installment debts as agreed. In such instances a particularly stubborn collection-loss situation can make an investor *wish* it were merely a vacancy. For obvious reasons each of the above criteria are considered to be of equal importance, and the omission or unavailability of any one item should make the owner/manager wary about giving possession of an expensive investment property to someone on the basis of one month's rent and minor deposit monies. In skeptical cases you may elect to contact your local retail credit association. This procedure is followed by all local business people whenever the smallest amount of installment credit is being requested. It will ordinarily be sufficient to obtain visual proof of large national or regional credit references, such as VISA, Master Charge, American Express, Carte Blanche, Shell, Exxon, Standard, and so on since these mammoth organizations rarely reveal information to individual inquirers. With prospective tenants who have scanty credit histories, you must rely upon local retail credit references, payment histories with local utility companies, consumer loans, etc. Local references can often be checked directly with local merchants, such as furniture stores, appliance centers, car dealers, realty companies, or other small businesses. Whatever the reference, it must be verifiable. It is often an error to accept the individual who boasts of paying cash for everything because of a philosophical distrust or dislike of credit. Such "individualists" should be seriously considered only when the other three criteria are considered acceptable *and* perhaps when they are able to pay the first and last months' rent and required deposits *in advance*. The real liability in accepting credit-free individuals is that they are also likely to be judgment-free—that is, they could become seriously delinquent in paying the rent, and, perhaps out of the adversary relationship that the "indignant tenant" is apt to precipitate, the apartment could be seriously damaged and finally abandoned, and not one dime would ever be collected. A local banker once told a "cash-only" acquaintance that there are three kinds of credit: good credit, bad credit, and no credit at all. The worst credit reference to have is no credit at all!

VERIFICATION OF STATED INCOME

The second most important variable in attempting to objectively select a tenant who will pay as agreed and reasonably occupy and use your leveraged property as expected is the formal verification of the stated source and amount of income. Verification must typically be done during conventional business hours and will usually be done by telephone and therefore be somewhat unofficial. In calling an employer, for instance, it is suggested that you ask for the immediate supervisor rather than make inquiries of the telephone receptionist. Brief and casual conversation with the immediate supervisor may allow you to draw some inferences about the character and reliability of the prospective tenant. In contrast, persons who are being subsidized by a social agency such as Social Security, public welfare, disability insurance, and so on will always have an assigned representative who can be contacted. One of the distinctions is that you cannot expect much information unless you deliver a signed release-of-information form to the assigned representative. Public and private agencies are extremely protective of "confidential" information about their clients. Caution must be exercised to avoid a possible discrimination complaint for arbitrarily rejecting someone on the basis of income alone or source of income alone. Subsidized tenants may be exceptionally reliable and desirable *if* they can afford the inflationary utility and rental rates. The recommended way to avoid accidental or even blatant discrimination on the basis of income is to consistently apply the same standards of selection for all tenants.

RULE OF FOUR-TO-ONE

The rule of Four-to-One requires the gross income to be at least four times the amount of the current rent. When consistently applied to all prospective tenants, this rule will almost always be supported in court if a tenant's rejections should be legally challenged. The weakest position for the owner/manager would be to have *no* consistent screening procedure. The rule of Four-to-One is based on the rational assumption that an individual cannot reasonably pay out more than 25% of his/her gross income for rent alone. It would be unrealistic to assume that a person with an $800-per-month gross income could afford to pay $300 per month in rent as well as all utilities and other day-to-day living expenses.

VERIFICATION OF FORMER RENTAL HISTORY

There will be many occasions when it is not practical or possible to evaluate a prospective tenant's rental history. Many young persons have never rented before. Some applicants are from out of state. In some situations the former owner/manager is simply unavailable. Whenever possible, it is a good strategy to contact the former owner/manager by telephone and casually inquire about your prospective tenant. Ask such questions as: "Did they pay the rent as agreed?" "Were there any problems?" "Would you recommend them to us as good renters?" Occasionally you might consider an inquiry with a neighbor of the prospective tenant. Neighbors are often keenly aware of annoying forms of behavior, such as frequent late parties, excessive noise, obnoxious pets, etc. Be very careful about being too snoopy. Respect each person's right to privacy and be prepared to drop or change a subject quickly if you sense any resentment or defensiveness. The sometimes difficult task to keep in mind is to quickly identify and accept the best possible tenant at a particular point in time and without violating someone's civil rights or the right to privacy.

VERIFICATION OF PERSONAL REFERENCES

Personal references are requested on virtually all written rental applications and credit applications. Typically, the prospective tenant will list only those personal friends and/or relatives whom they assume will say only positive things about them. Nominally, the references are being requested as a sign of stability in the community and perhaps to "trace" someone or forward mail if the tenant moves unexpectedly. In practice, there can be more value in verifying personal references than in just obtaining a forwarding address. Assumed "friends" will often reveal things about their friends which they might not expect. By keeping the conversation casual and by asking only non-controversial and indirect questions, it is often quite surprising what will be "volunteered."

SAMPLE RENTAL AGREEMENT

THIS AGREEMENT, entered into in _____(city)_____, _____(state)_____ on this_____ day of_____, 19_____, by and between (business name, etc.),AS PRINCIPALS and/or ASSIGNED REPRESENTATIVES and _____ hereinafter called respectively lessor and lessee. In consideration of the payment of rents and specific performances as contained in this agreement, lessor does hereby rent to lessee for use as a residence the premises located at_____, _____(city)_____, __(state & zip code)__, on a month-to-month lease commencing on the_____day of_____, 19_____, and at the monthly rental of $_____, payable in advance on the _____day of each and every month.

It is further mutually agreed between the parties that:

1. The above premises shall be occupied by no more than _____ adults and _____ children and _____ pets as a residence only.
2. Lessee shall not violate any city ordinance or state law in or about the above premises.
3. Lessee shall not sublet the above premises or assign this agreement without the lessor's written consent.
4. Lessee shall keep and maintain the above premises in a clean and orderly condition at all times and upon termination of the tenancy shall surrender the premises to the lessor in approximately the same condition as when received. A cleaning and damage fee of $_____ is to be paid in advance and $ _____ of same is to be returned if the premises are returned in a clean and orderly condition and all payments have been made promptly as agreed.
5. Tenancy of the dwelling may be terminated by either party, by giving 30 days' written notice to the other party. Further, if rent is unpaid within the agreed-upon due dates, lessor will issue lessee a 24-hour notice to pay the rent in full or vacate the premises. Failure to do either can result in a court-ordered eviction and/or judgment.
6. The lessor shall pay for all garbage collection, water, sewer, exterior electricity, fire insurance (excluding tenant possessions), management, and all approved maintenance repairs.
7. Lessee hereby waives all rights to make repairs at expense of the lessor.
8. Lessee shall pay for all gas, light, heat, power, telephone service, and all other services, except as herein provided, which are sup-

plied to the above premises. Lessee should provide own insurance for possessions.

9. Lessor shall not be responsible or liable for loss or damage to property that belongs to the lessee, or is located in or near the dwelling, when such loss is not clearly the result of lessor's negligence.

10. Lessor reserves the right to enter and/or inspect the premises upon reasonable notice and/or in cases of apparent emergencies, and to show the premises to prospective tenants after notice of intention to vacate has been given. Lessee agrees to permit repair persons on the premises to make any repairs or any improvements deemed necessary by the lessor.

11. Lessee agrees to pay a $10 charge for any returned check and/or a $10 late fee for any rent payment made after midnight of the last day of the agreed-upon payment period.

12. Special terms and conditions (if any): _____

_____

_____

In signing this agreement lessee acknowledges that he and/or she has completely read, understands, and will abide by the terms of this agreement; further, that this agreement has been prepared in duplicate on the date indicated above and a copy has been received by lessee.

_____ _____
Tenant-Lessee   Owner-Lessor

THE MOVE-IN CHECKLIST

It is most important that a new tenant complete a Move-In Checklist *prior* to allowing him and/or her to move in their possessions. The rationale is very simply that some damage (sometimes serious damage) will often occur during the process of moving into a rental unit. Additional damage (other than "normal wear and tear") will often occur during each tenant's occupancy. Such damage will invariably be attributed to the "former tenant" when the current tenant vacates the rental unit.

Unless a signed and dated Move-In Checklist can be produced, it is simply the tenant's word against the owner's in any attempt to "prove" who is responsible for any damage which exceeds "normal wear and tear." A typical Move-In Checklist can be adequately made up by the owner/manager and printed in reasonable quantities to be used with all future tenants. The checklist should allow space to write in (or check off) detailed information about *each* room, such as the condition of the walls, ceiling, floor (and/or floor covering), doors, windows, appliances, draperies, etc. Items needing repair can be acknowledged and/or repaired by the owner/manager. The potential for argument about the refund of cleaning and/or damage fees will be substantially reduced. So will the amount of accidental or intentional damage that can be passed on to the "former tenants."

AVOIDING LATE RENT PAYMENTS

Most of the late rental payments can be avoided by setting a firm and enforcible policy with each tenant prior to occupancy and by consistent follow-through. It is imperative to first learn what you can about the local statutes applicable to landlord-tenant relations, especially when and how to define, serve notice, and apply legal remedies in cases of delinquent payment. Avoid complications and possible counter-suits by remaining strictly legal. A policy statement should be prepared in written form to advise new tenants exactly when and where to pay the rent, the required method of paying (*e.g.*, check or money order), how to address the rent payment, when it is considered to be late, and the consequences of a late rental payment (*e.g.*, a $10. late fee and/or a 24-hour notice to pay the rent in full or vacate the premises).

In most areas there is a 10-day grace period in which the monthly rental is to be paid. After approximately 5 to 8 days, it may be appropriate to issue a *reminder notice* that the current rental payment has not yet been received. Another strategy is to insist upon payment of the rent by check or money order only. This procedure helps to eliminate much of the game-playing that can occur as "excuses" for not paying the monthly rental on time. In states where the law requires a 10-day grace period in the payment of the rent, it is usually standard practice to issue a 24-*hour notice* to the delinquent tenant to pay the rent in full or vacate the premises within that time limit. This procedure will generally elicit a distinct response. If not, the next procedure is to apply at the county courthouse for a Forceable Entry and Detainer (F.E.D.) to have the tenant legally removed. In a matter of days a representative from the county courthouse or county sheriff's office will deliver a subpoena to the delinquent tenant which sets a date for both the plaintiff and the defendant to appear in small-claims court for a hearing. Most obstinate tenants will either pay the overdue rent or vacate the premises prior to the date for appearance in court. This full procedure often takes 3 or 4 weeks to complete, and it is possible that no rental monies will ever be collected. Judgments against a tenant (credit-poor or not) do not mean much when he/she cannot be located or has few material assets. Failure to act promptly and legally in a delinquent rent situation can result in months of unrecoverable rent payments. One final comment along these lines is to never "carry" a delinquent tenant on the basis of a verbal agreement only. Subject to subtle variations in the law from one area to another, the thing to tell a delinquent tenant who says it will not be possible to pay the rent until later in the month is: "It is not possible for me to extend credit without a written agreement and a security deposit which is at least equal to the amount of rent that is owed." The conscientious tenant with the situational difficulty will tend to accept this offer. The potential "deadbeat" who has no real intention of paying the delinquent rent tends to be "smoked out." The proper handling of such situations can substantially improve the satisfaction that is realized by the individual owner and/or manager.

TENANT RIGHTS

All parts of the country have been experiencing rapid change in the legal definition of tenant rights. The well-organized civil rights movements and the consumer rights movements have been uncommonly effective in altering the "landlord-tenant relationship." The courts have typically favored tenants to a much greater degree and have been typically harsh in restricting the real and imagined "abuses" of "landlords," "slumlords," "absentee owners," "property barons," and the like. The legal message that is being communicated is that both landlord and tenant must be aware of local, state, and federal regulations in their particular area. Most of the recent and ongoing legislation and laws relating to landlord-tenant rights is confined to four basic areas: (1) minimum housing quality standards; (2) contract law; (3) rent-control regulations; and (4) anti-discrimination laws. Periodic review and some study of the relevant landlord-tenant laws will be necessary if an investor is to avoid potentially time-consuming and/or expensive legal complications. The most likely sources of "survival information" regarding local landlord-tenant laws would include your personal attorney and broker, media summaries of recent court cases, apartment owners' associations, and legal materials that can be obtained from municipal and state regulatory agencies. A brief summary of the four basic areas of concern would be as follows:

1. Minimum Housing Quality Standards

The primary obligation of the lessor in providing space for residential purposes is an implied warranty of habitability and general freedom from building code violations. State and local governments have enacted substantial regulations to ensure minimum livability standards to protect the health and safety of tenants in residential properties. These regulations are typically administered by city/county building inspectors, fire inspectors, and housing or health inspectors. The principal areas of concern in residential rental units relate to minimum standards for such things as adequate heating, plumbing, and electrical systems, as well as provision of "basic shelter." The concept of basic shelter implies freedom from exposure to the elements—protection from unsanitary conditions, protection from rain and excessive coldness, protection of privacy and basic security (*e.g.*, secure locks to minimize possible sexual assault, or unwanted entry to the residential unit). Individual codes may also set standards for room sizes, clearances, accessibility, ventilation, fire alarm and detection devices, insulation, electric outlets and lighting, and so on. Failure to abide by these minimum standards can result in costly insurance liability exemptions in the case of a lawsuit and/or a possible legal defense in a tenant's refusal to pay delinquent rent and prevent eviction on the grounds that conditions of the premises represent a violation of the implied warranty of habitability.

2. Contract Law

The long-standing doctrine of *caveat emptor* (let the buyer beware) no longer has much applicability to the landlord-tenant relationship. In its place most communities have enacted complex statutes which have substantially redefined the landlord-tenant relationship. National and local court decisions have significantly shaped the "legalistic" aspects of that relationship. The "landlord" must now follow a formally prescribed, time-consuming, and ritualistic procedure to evict a delinquent tenant. The legal concept of suing for "specific performance" requires that a set of specific elements be demonstrated. Is the written agreement that exists binding? Has there been a specific failure in performance? Has reasonable notice been served? Are there specific damages? Such questions apply especially to leases, rental agreements, service or employment contracts, verbal promises, or any specific issue which may involve the rights and obligations of landlord and tenant. Clear guidelines can often be maintained only with the assistance of a personal attorney. Most legalistic documents and basic legal matters are "adequate" until there is a distinct problem. The investor who seeks the highest margin of profit and lowest margin of time loss in legalistic situations will do everything possible to avoid the deterioration of a written agreement and use the most binding possible agreement when legal remedies might be sought.

3. Rent Control Regulations

The sustained pressure on individual household budgets as a result of high-interest rates, inflation, increased taxes, and spotty unemployment rates has accentuated the demand for rent controls in many communities. Recent "tax rebellions" have also stimulated the demand for rent controls in response to investors' "windfall profits." The historical failures of rent-control regulations have done little to stifle this "popular notion of income redistribution." Governments of Sweden, Holland, and Great Britain, and major cities such as Paris and New York have all tried rent controls with varying degrees of failure. In general, rent controls severely restrict interest in producing new units, existing units decline in number and quality because of maintenance dis-incentives, shortages occur, and changing population pressures severely distort the basic land-use patterns. Continuous legal battles must be waged to adjust income to expenses. In New York City a study of 2,400 units with rent control indicated that from 1971 to 1976 operating costs increased 57.4% while gross rents increased only 35.3%. Property owners must typically present financial statements to designated review boards to justify any rent increase. The procedure is intentionally slow and frustrating. The increases that are eventually approved are usually restricted to a percentage of the total gross income. The situation is further complicated by a variety of exceptions, such as small owner-occupied apartment buildings, units built after a specified date, apartments occupied by members of the owner's family, and increases in rent as a result of tenant turnover. The long-term effects can be most unsatisfactory, yet politically unfeasible to remove. Ultimately, government must heavily subsidize rents and construction.

4. Anti-Discrimination Laws

Human perceptions and behaviors continuously change. In the area of housing discrimination, there have been radical amounts of change since the impetus that resulted in Title VIII of the Civil Rights Act of 1968. That "Act" specified that it would be unlawful to discriminate against any individual because of identification with a particular ethnic background, religion, or national origin in the sale or rental of housing, advertising, financing, or the provision of real estate brokerage services. The real estate "industry" as a whole was pitifully slow in complying with this legislated mandate to change. After 10 full years of court cases, changing economic realities, and vastly improved perceptions of persons with a "different" background, the real estate "industry" as a whole has been making frequent, significant, and genuine contributions to the needed civil rights movement. That "movement" has gained substantial strength over the past 10 years, in particular, and now may be considered to relate to a prohibition of discrimination on the basis of any single-factor dimension. In most areas of the country, it is forbidden to discriminate solely on the basis of age, sex, sexual orientation, physical handicap, or other factor which arbitrarily excludes an entire "class" of people. For instance, arbitrary rejection of an individual because she receives Aid to Dependent Children (A.D.C.) has been found to be an example of sex discrimination, because virtually all persons receiving A.D.C. are female. Architectural barriers which discriminate against the mobility-impaired should be removed in all instances which do not represent overwhelming financial hardships. Discrimination on the basis of marital status is unnecessary and unenforceable. Regrettably, in most areas of the country there are no formal prohibitions to prevent discrimination against prospective tenants with children. This offensive practice of segregating persons with children from persons without children creates an unnatural environment with economic and psychological hardships for the children, in particular. Two years ago there was a local example of inconsistency in the application of the "no kids" rule. A federal jury awarded a financial settlement to an interracial couple who claimed they were evicted from their apartment largely because the husband was black. The defendants had argued that the couple was evicted because they had violated a section of the rental agreement which prohibited children as residents of the apartment complex. The plaintiffs convincingly argued that other children were living in the apartment complex and that the management was aware of the child's presence for several months before the notice of rental termination was served. Discrimination against low-income persons is ultimately expensive for very large portions of the community. If a prospective tenant's income is below the rule of Four to One, other alternatives must be considered, such as a lower-priced unit, a smaller unit, increasing the number of rent-paying individuals per unit, government subsidies, and related. The owner/manager goal in selecting tenants can be to screen out the chronic delinquent, not necessarily the low-income person who may possess a high degree of reliability. Approximately 25% to 50% of the month-to-month, rent-paying residents of any community can be described as elderly, disabled, or low-income individuals. They deserve an opportunity in the community. They cannot be ignored.

AVOIDING TENANT EVICTION

Don't be too quick to evict. A better strategy is to negotiate minor delinquencies of the rent to resolve possible difficulties in a friendly and courteous manner. Allow an extra day or two beyond the strict legal definition of rental delinquency. The reasons for being occasionally late with the rent are too diverse to even make a meaningful generalization about them. Valid or not, this is one of the petty nuisances that all property managers must relate to periodically. The conscientious renter who is temporarily delinquent can usually be differentiated from the renter who is about to become (or previously has been) chronically delinquent and a tough adversary for extended periods of time. Since this is not always true, the typically successful property manager will have firm guidelines about the "tolerable" period of rental delinquency and a thorough knowledge of the local procedures to follow through with a formal eviction and/or collection process.

Improperly handled tenant evictions will be complex, time-consuming, frustrating, and a virtual "no-win" situation for the income-property manager. The whole process of tenant eviction (an unpopular legal action in the public's mind) has been undergoing substantial change as consumer-protection legislation continues to accumulate in each state's body of statutory law. In all fairness, the legislative intent has been to correct the *genuine* and the assumed abuses of the past. The spotlighted emphasis upon "landlord-tenant" relations has resulted in tough laws which are beneficial to both parties, but are predominantly in favor of the tenant. The tenant, as a consumer of essential housing services, is represented by powerful coalitions of special-interest groups—consumer-protection groups, subsidized income groups, organizations for the handicapped, minority groups, legal-aid attorneys, "Gray Panthers," and so on. These lobbyists (often coalitions of lobbyists) have been overwhelmingly effective in obtaining expanded tenant protections under the law. In the absence of effective counter-lobbying, the legal position of the income-property owner/manager has been steadily eroded. The fee-based attorneys representing property owners and the often busy property owners themselves typically cannot financially afford to personally lobby for well-written legislation that clearly represents the best interests of both parties. Under the present circumstances, "landlords" tend to be grossly under-represented and frequently stereotyped as "tax-evading, greedy capitalists" in these legislative sessions across the nation. The outcome of this extensive new consumer-oriented legislation is that a mutually binding "legal partnership" has been established between property owners and tenants which precisely defines what can and cannot be done.* The tenant who could be readily bluffed, intimidated, and further abused by the district courts is mostly a thing of the past. Contemporary tenants have ready access to legal counseling, and a vast repertoire of legal defenses,

---

*See, for example, Goodman, Emily J., *Tenant Survival Book,* New York: Bobbs-Merrill Co., 1974; also, Marcus, Michael H., *Landlord-Tenant Relations for Oregon,* Vancouver, B.C., Self-Counsel Press Inc., 1978.

counter-claims, and remedies. The "landlord" will typically prevail in a court of law if allowed sufficient time. The issues are time and collectability. The litigation process (including the legal defense of real and/or contrived counter-claims) will be excruciatingly long and tedious. In the meantime, rents likely will not be paid and maintenance costs will tend to increase dramatically in response to the bitter adversary relationship that tends to develop between the rival parties. The owner must routinely satisfy all monthly obligations as if nothing unusual had occurred. The big distinction between the two parties is that the property-owner can readily have a judgment placed against his or her property, whereas the highly mobile tenant (even with reasonable credit references) remains largely, if not completely, judgment-free. The net effect is that the property owner/manager would usually prefer to cut the inevitable losses and virtually beg for a mutual release of all further claims ("Judgment by Stipulation") by each party and to gain possession of the disputed property at some mutually agreed-upon time. At its worst, this can be the kind of collection loss that can make an income-property owner/manager desperate for the possession of an ordinary vacancy! Mistakes in this area should be anticipated and avoided. Consult your personal attorney before overreacting to the "rightness" of your particular claims. If you must evict a tenant, do everything properly.

The technical elements of a court-ordered tenant eviction will vary from one legal jurisdiction to another and with time. The basic requirements for an expeditious and ideally uncomplicated court-ordered eviction (also known as a "Forcible Entry and Detainer," or F.E.D.) would be approximately as follows:

1. Literally study and comply with the local statutes regarding the required formal steps of the eviction process (consult your personal attorney if not familiar with the full process).

2. In making the decision to initiate the eviction process, the property manager must demonstrate a sufficient and lawful cause. Common examples would be non-payment of rent, intended or actual sale of the property, or merely the lawful desire

to regain possession of the property. Eviction can *never* be in retaliation for reasonable maintenance demands (health, safety, or general habitability concerns), as a form of unlawful discrimination, in violation of federally subsidized housing standards, or in violation of a verbal or written rental agreement.

3. Formal notice of the intended eviction must be in writing, properly addressed and dated, and fully describe the conditions of the intended eviction. A standardized form (*e.g.*, 24-hour notice, Eviction for Cause, Eviction for Irreparable Damage, Eviction for Non-Payment of Rent, etc.) which is available from a legal-stationery supply, your real estate broker, or your personal attorney should be used. Keep it simple. Type in only what information that is necessary and retain multiple copies.

4. Proper delivery of the signed eviction notice is critical. Failure to prove that the eviction notice was actually delivered to the appropriate party (defective notice) will result in the dismissal of the legal action. To prevent this, always use at least two means of delivery for the eviction notice. The notice can be delivered in person whenever this is possible. Even then an additional copy should be sent in the conventional mail. Typically, if the tenant is not readily available, one copy should be sent by certified (return receipt requested) mail and another copy sent by conventional mail. Never proceed with further legal action until you have personal evidence that the notice was received.

5. Assuming that the tenant does not respond to the formal eviction notice by voluntarily moving, the property manager will have to file a specified complaint (F.E.D. or related name) at the county courthouse. A relatively nominal filing fee must be paid, plaintiff and defendants identified, and two copies of the eviction notice (and proof of delivery) attached to the complaint.

6. The next step is for a civil process deputy or authorized county representative to serve the notice to the identified tenant either in person or by securely attaching the notice to the tenant's door. Both plaintiff and defendant will be notified of a time and place to appear for a preliminary hearing to set a future trial date.

If the tenant fails to appear, the judgment will be granted. If the property manager fails to appear, the complaint will be dismissed. At the time of this hearing, the presiding judge will typically ask each party if they want to be represented by an attorney and whether or not they want to have a jury trial.

With highly litigious tenants, this may be the ideal time to attempt a negotiated settlement ("out in the hallway"). The purpose would be to mutually agree to sign an agreement in which all present claims and any further counter-claims would be dropped on the condition that the property be vacated within a reasonably defined time.

7. If all efforts to provide a negotiated settlement are unsuccessful, it will be necessary to appear in court to obtain a legal decision on the enforcibility of the intended eviction. The property manager who has done everything in a responsible and lawful manner will invariably prevail. However, the potential for "trumped-up" and/or legitimate counter-claims should be anticipated and you should be advised by and/or actually represented by your personal attorney. In all cases the judge will allow the tenant a reasonable period of time to obtain new housing (at least 10 to 14 days). The concern for collectibility of delinquent rent and possible damages is an entirely separate issue and will tend to be a moot point.

9

Rental-Property Maintenance and General Management

Maintenance and repair of rental units, as opposed to liquidity, are probably the toughest issues for each investor to resolve before feeling comfortable about assuming responsibilities for income-producing properties. Maintenance and repair are the primary characteristics of income-producing properties which separate the wishful thinkers from the actual performers. Newspapers and other popular "literature" contain frequent examples of real and satirical horror stories about the pitfalls of rental-property and personal-property maintenance. There will inevitably be some exaggerations about maintenance "problems" which will scare off the curious and uncommitted. Example: one local investor in restorable mansions will not consider a 50-to-100-unit apartment building with a comparable amount of investment capital, because in that person's mind there are 50 to 100 toilets that are stopped up and overflowing at the same time! The potential for problems and complaints does increase with the size of the investment, but not necessarily in a proportionate manner. The important distinction to be made about increased investment size is that potential profits and resources to cope with problems usually increase at a very acceptable rate. Maintenance and repair can be, and usually are, an ongoing expense that is reasonably predictable and reliable and can be creatively "averaged" over the life of the investment.

The reluctant investor who possesses an aversion to "other people's dirt" will do well to consider professional management, one or more employees, or some other form of investment. There are fortunes being made in effectively handling other people's dirt! Whether you do it yourself or pay someone else to do it—prompt and efficient cleaning of other people's dirt is a major component of the success in handling income-producing properties. Most people are offended by the sight of another person's dirt, especially when they will be taking possession of that particular living unit. In many instances maintenance and repair of any unit refers primarily to the need to do a thorough job of *cleaning* the unit and its surroundings.

Anticipatory maintenance and repair are major factors in the investor's analysis of a property and the decision to proceed, negotiate, or abandon a particular project. Anticipatory maintenance and repair will include estimates of the cost of initial upgrading, deferred maintenance, ongoing maintenance, and changes necessary prior to sale of the property. Throughout this private evaluation process, the price, terms, and economic outlook will generally be the prime factors in a personal decision to continue the evaluation, or seek other investment opportunities. Maintenance and repair are significantly variable expense items which must be predicted with a fairly high degree of accuracy to determine true market values and the potential rates of return. Maintenance and repair which are frequently elusive and/or disguised variables—which include known, deferrable, and unknown problems—are commonly referred to as *deferred maintenance*. Major errors of judgment in the area of deferred maintenance can substantially alter the percentage of return on investment—especially in the short term. A local investor purchased a well-constructed, English Tudor-style fraternity house in a small college town. The basic intent was to convert it into a profitable group home or multiple-family dwelling. Within the first 30 days of ownership, the archaic heating system broke down and had to be replaced. This particular heating system was a one-of-a-kind, handmade furnace. The cost of replacement, which could no longer be traced to the seller since there was no such warranty in the sale agreement, was approximately $7,000, and this nearly caused the unsuspecting new owner to lose this "investment." Situations such as the one just described can be largely corrected through perceptive evaluation practices *and* written stipulations in the purchase agreement that major appliances such as heating systems, air-conditioning systems, plumbing, and electrical systems are accepted subject to professional inspection and/or guaranteed against major defect for a period of 14 days, 30 days, 90 days, etc. Assistance can be obtained from your personal attorney in writing such a simple and binding agreement into the earnest money agreement *before* you sign.

Invariably, a building which is priced at or below current market values will need cleaning and new paint both inside and out. It is for this particular reason that you may be able to bargain effectively for a good price, good terms, or both. Defects of appearance (not structural problems) are especially conspicuous during the cold, wet, or snowy winter days when a poor appearance is not easily correctible. If windows are cracked, broken, or drafty, exterior siding damaged, floor tiles broken, carpet excessively worn, foundation and steps seriously cracked, and the roofing material currently blowing onto the neighbor's property, you might anticipate considerable expense—if you consider it at all! The knowledgeable investor would incorporate the cost of these repairs (not just material costs) in his/her first and perhaps a second bid upon a given property. One of the investor's shrewdest bargaining powers is derived from the *mutual awareness* of unavoidable repair and replacement costs both in terms of materials and the time necessary to make the repairs. The "handyman special" is not such a bargain if the investor grossly underestimates his/her own time, effort, and degree of skill required in making the necessary restorations. The "fixer-upper" may even be disastrous if the investor fails to recognize the true extent of the problems. One mark of a successful investor is the ability to recognize the intangible flaws which are essential to making an appropriate decision to accept, reject, or modify the terms of a given piece of income-producing property. There is far less disgrace in rejecting a property which would have been sufficiently profitable than there is in accepting a property which is essentially unprofitable.

The traditionally difficult and least tangible types of deferred maintenance are in the broad areas which cannot be readily evaluated by casual observation. An approximate (non-inclusive) list would be as follows:

1. Water Problems
    a. Improper drainage of rainwater away from the foundation
    b. Occasionally improper drainage to the sewer or septic tank
    c. Rusty, corroded, inaccessible waterpipes, drains, and valves
    d. Leaky, overly damp basement or crawlspace
    e. Condensation build-up in attic due to inadequate ventilation
    f. Leaky roof, windowsills, doorjambs, or waterpipes
    g. Rotted wood due to exposure to water or damp soil

2. Insulation Problems
    a. Ceiling, walls, and flooring inadequately insulated (evaluate on a cold day; previous fuel bills can be very unreliable)
    b. Waterpipes and furnace pipes improperly insulated
    c. Absence of storm doors and storm windows (especially in northern states; absence of air-conditioning units in "sun belt" states)
    d. Main entrance and living area faces coldest, northerly direction
    e. Trees and windbreaks improperly placed, wrong type, overgrown
    f. Inefficient furnace, exorbitant or concealed heating bills
    g. "Total electric home"

3. Structural Problems
    a. Significant cracks or other improper signs of settling
    b. Uneven floors, out-of-square doorways, or sagging roof line
    c. Inferior materials or construction techniques
    d. Cosmetic cover-ups (*e.g.*, fresh paint or stucco over concrete)
    e. Dry rot, termites, carpenter ants, fire damage, unfinished work

164 Real Estate Investment

    f. Rooms too small, "illegal," awkwardly arranged or missing
    g. Architectural barriers
    h. Inadequate exits in case of fire or other emergency

4. Hardware Problems
   a. Inadequate electrical systems, cheap fixtures, missing fixtures
   b. Corroded, obsolete plumbing fixtures, inadequate drains
   c. Worn, inadequate locks, doorknobs, switches, hinges, etc.
   d. Worn-out appliances such as stove and refrigerator, washer and dryer, hot-water tank, baseboard heaters, garbage disposal, etc.

5. Miscellaneous Problems
   a. Zoning restrictions, nuisance problems, undesirable pending changes
   b. Possible easement problems, encroachment
   c. Tax assessment about to be increased substantially
   d. Noise pollution, inadequate parking facilities, limited privacy
   e. Pest problems, pet problems, odor problems
   f. Falsified tenant records or maintenance records

To minimize or resolve many of the hazards indicated above, there must be more than a casual on-site inspection. This may become progressively more difficult as the number of units increases. However, it is important to actually study as much of the physical structure as possible. If you will only be able to fully inspect a "representative" unit such as the manager's unit or a currently vacant unit, be especially cautious. Consider a thorough inspection of at *least* one or more additional units which are selected totally at random. Be imaginative. Evaluate the property under the harshest possible conditions, such as extreme cold, wind, and rain if at all possible. Observe the noise and congestion levels during the rush hours. Make daytime and evening observations. *Casually* chat with neighbors, tenants, and perhaps a former owner. Research the county records for the history of tax assessment, history of deeds, zoning, and related. Investigate the recent history of real estate listings if possible.

Some items which should be verified independently from what the seller reports are: cost of insurance for the new owner, cost of garbage collection, cost of water, sewer, and other utilities. Use a checklist to be aware of possible omissions. Always protect yourself by structuring any earnest money agreement to include "subject to . . ." or "in lieu of . . ." clauses. Example: "In lieu of formal inspection by municipal building inspector . . ." "Subject to formal inspection by a licensed electrical contractor . . ." "In lieu of formal inspection by a professional pest exterminator . . ." "Subject to review and approval of personal attorney . . ." "Subject to approval for conventional financing . . ." So you can *kill* a bad deal.

To keep reality in perspective, it should possibly be stressed that absolute perfection is not the usual goal. A rental property will rarely, if ever, be at its optimum level of general maintenance and repair at all times. Assuming that typical repairs are made at the time of acquisition, maintenance is usually an ongoing concern which can be staggered over the economic life of the investment. "Surprises" can generally be kept under control. Major maintenance—for example, new roofing material—typically does not have to be resolved immediately, and a variety of decisions can be made regarding the best time, method, and cost to be considered.

Without exception, the most important part of investment-property maintenance is skillful and timely cleaning of the property to be rented. The basic skills and equipment required to do an acceptable job vary little from the items used in a rigorous "spring cleaning" of your own residence. When possible have everything cleared out first. An empty dwelling is substantially easier to clean than a furnished one. Most persons already possess the basic knowledge and personal experience to effectively clean the interior and exterior of an apartment or a single-family dwelling. A variety of ordinary cleaning detergents, carpet shampooers, floor waxers, "flea bombs," deodorizers, etc., are on the market and do not necessarily need to be purchased in unusually large quantities or be of "industrial strength." The basic requirement is that individual effort and attention be given to the ceilings, walls, floors, fixtures, windows, doors, and appliances to remove conspicuous dirt, grease, stains, cobwebs, odors, pests, and debris. Irregardless of age or basic condition of the property, a unit is rentable if it has been personally cleaned and inspected to the best of your ability prior to being inspected by the first prospective tenants. It is this writer's personal recommendation that a rental property should never be offered in a dirty or run-down condition. It is reckless folly to offer a discount on the rent, such as the first month's rent, in exchange for cleaning the unit. The rationale for this recommendation is as follows:

1. You're in the investment business to make a maximum lawful return on your original investment.
2. The appearance of an untidy rental property can possibly cause you to lose the meticulous, fastidious renter who would routinely keep the property in a more desirable condition.
3. The discounted tenant may or may not actually clean (and/or repair) the property, and, learning from the example set before occupancy, they will invariably leave the property in the same undesirable condition upon vacating the premises.
4. You are denying yourself a cleaning fee which provides some incentive for the tenant to leave the property in approximately the same condition as when it was first entered. The cleaning fee and/or damage fee are crucial screening criteria in obtaining a financially reliable tenant.

Whenever possible, the time to clean a rental unit is prior to the time it is first shown. A vacant unit is substantially easier to clean thoroughly than one which is full of furniture and other possessions. The amount of rent lost in having a rental unit vacant for a few days is inconsequential compared to the losses that could occur as a result of offering a poorly cleaned or just plain dirty rental unit. How long would you expect a used-car dealer to remain in business if the dealer made no effort to clean and recondition automobiles before showing them? Thorough cleaning will likely reveal much about the need for additional redecoration, repair, and future replacement of various objects and enable you to formulate decisions about probable dates to make necessary improvements. Cleaning, like redecoration and remodeling, can often be done economically by the investor and perhaps with the help of the investor's family or temporarily hired employees. An investor can hire temporary help without all the hassles of withholding taxes, social security taxes, and worker's compensation by hiring the "private contractors" who *advertise* their labor services in the local newspaper. Such individuals are responsible for their own withholding records and accident insurance.

PREVENTATIVE MAINTENANCE

Preventative maintenance begins prior to the acquisition of the investment property. Accurate detection and assessment of hidden or deferred-maintenance problems may avoid some very difficult financial surprises. The extra cost of creatively doing the research or of obtaining some "expert" opinions can be worth every dollar. Various "experts" might include bank appraisors, building inspectors, electrical or plumbing inspectors, surveyors, pest inspectors, and so on. A precedent-setting legal case occurred in the state of Massachusetts many years ago in which a home buyer sued the seller for damages when it was discovered that the dwelling was severely damaged by termites. The ruling of the court was that the defendant had not told the plaintiff that there were *not* termites in the dwelling! Compare the ancient concept of *caveat emptor.*

Personal skills in assessing problems within a particular area and of resolving many of them as they occur improve as an investor acquires experience with specific properties. Experience helps to minimize the chance of becoming aware of a financially disastrous maintenance problem after the fact. The services of a "professional" should be utilized when feasible to establish a possible "escape clause," a more effective bargaining position, or at least a more informed and less biased opinion than your own and the seller's. These selected opinions can be in addition to your own educated judgment. An entry-leval example might be where a novice investor with little capital to risk in speculation relies heavily upon V.A. and/or F.H.A. assessments of current market value, maintenance needs, and minimal acceptable standards for habitation. The limitation of this method is that F.H.A. rules prohibit an owner-occupant from obtaining F.H.A. financing more frequently than once every two years. Also, a non-resident "investor" must pay at least 10% to 15% *more* on the down payment to obtain F.H.A. financing. Regional changes in the "rules" should be carefully watched.

A likely place to begin trying to assess liabilities and potential maintenance needs of a particular piece of property is with a thorough inspection of the land upon which it is located. Consider the following:

1. Is the investment property well situated with respect to other buildings, hills, valleys, streams, highways, and mixed zoning areas?

2. Is the prospective investment property well located on high, sloping, or level ground? Pay special attention to shallow areas, land which slopes toward the foundation, underground springs, poor drainage areas, potential flood areas, or unusually high water tables.

3. Inspect the foundation carefully. Only a continuous concrete foundation should be acceptable. Carry a medium-sized screwdriver or a pocket knife during the inspection so you can use the blunt end for tapping (some concrete facings are only a facade) and the sharp end for probing suspect timbers or joists which may have dry rot or termites. Evaluate any significant flaws in the concrete (virtually all concrete has minor fractures that do not represent a problem). Large fractures may represent expensive settling and/or leakage problems. Without a sufficiently high, solid, and continuous concrete foundation, don't even consider it. Conventional banks and future buyers won't consider it, either! The eye can be deceived. You must train

yourself to look for the potential problems which could be overly expensive. Especially with older single-family dwellings, practice tapping the concrete gently in a variety of suspect places. It could be ¼-inch stucco over rotting wood! Use a strong light to inspect for unusual dampness, stains, cracks, insects, leaks, and new paint which may be covering defects. Watch for recent patch work or incongruent remodeling efforts which may be concealing an important defect. Enhance your perceptive and intuitive skills by conducting your inspection(s) and your offer(s) on a cold, wet, and windy day whenever possible.

THE IMPORTANCE OF PAINT

For most investors there are basically just two kinds of paint to be familiar with—latex and enamel. Many persons would argue that latex is the only acceptable paint because it is usually less expensive, water soluble, easier to clean up, faster drying, and odor free! All of these claims are basically true up to a point. In covering any exterior enamel, latex will tend to blister and peel within 1 to 36 months and may be most unattractive at the proposed time of sale. Instead of getting an average life-span of 5 to 6 years on a new coat of exterior paint, the new buyer may get only 1 year, or less! This reduced life-span of the paint may also affect the investor who acquires such a newly painted dwelling. The distinction in part is that enamel will allow a wood surface to "breathe," and latex will not. The result of placing exterior latex over exterior enamel will eventually be blisters. This dilemma can be resolved by consulting experts you can trust and by staying with "like kinds" of paint for exterior jobs. One way to determine if the exterior paint is an oil-base enamel or not is to rub it with your hand or a piece of cloth. If the paint is chalky and come off, it is an oil-base enamel.

Inside, latex paints are usually the most satisfactory and economical to use. Even the casual amateur can apply these easy-to-clean-up paints with a roller, brush, sponge-brush, or the very fast airless spray equipment. Latex paint will give the walls and ceiling in each room a clean and bright appearance. The use of very pale pastel colors and the many shades of "off-white" will probably give the best results. Intense colors are more apt to magnify a defect, make a room appear smaller, or "offend" the prospective renters who are trying to mentally color-coordinate their possessions with the existing color scheme. It is more than just chance that nearly all newer apartment buildings utilize "off-white" in every room except possibly the kitchen or bathroom.

It is this writer's opinion that under no circumstances should a prospective tenant, or even a long-term renter, be allowed to "paint it themselves." The gains to be made in time and labor will typically not equal the regrets of having an exceptionally poor or incomplete job done. Few renters are as competent in painting as they think they are. The distinction seems to be in the fact that it is substantially easier to think through a job than it is to actually do it. They paint the windows shut. They get paint on the electrical fixtures, doorknobs, woodwork, and all over the floor! The prudent manager will typically use a signed rental agreement which prohibits the tenants from ordering or providing any direct service to the property. Owner/managers should resist the temptation of "free labor" even when the tenant offers to provide everything except the materials. Interest diminishes rapidly when the tenant becomes frustrated and feels martyred in making improvements on someone else's property. As a successful property manager, you have not necessarily angered the tenant by consistently refusing his or her offer of service. Some exceptions may exist when an experienced tradesperson makes a knowledgeable offer to provide a specific service. In such cases the owner/manager can formally grant permission in advance and in writing to perform a well-defined task. This written agreement can resolve most of the possible "misunderstandings" which seem to occur and which can lead to legal battles and financial loss. In situations where there are cost overruns from the original estimates, the same process of written agreements can be followed and the owner/manager will maintain control over the situation to a maximum extent. The basic elements that should go into a written and signed agreement can be described as follows:

1. A full description of what is to be done and by whom may be very important if a dispute leads to a small-claims courtroom where the tenant is suing you because he or she "thought" you had authorized unlimited materials as long as they were providing "free labor." Such misunderstandings can be minimized when there is mutual planning between the lessor and the lessee before the over-zealous lessee rushes into complex jobs with the expectation that approval can be obtained after the fact.

2. By insisting upon an itemized description of materials to be used and the most competitive price per item *before* you make a decision, you maintain control in the situation and you keep the responsibility on the tenant to provide the details which are necessary to make an appropriate decision. The lessor retains the responsibility to reject any part or all of the itemized proposal. When the procrastinating tenant seems to keep the owner/manager on the defensive with frequent requests and ideas, the itemized list may never be completed. Insisting upon monotonous detail will likely discourage the well-meaning tenant whose motivation is already beginning to fade. The best protection, of course, is to avoid these situations entirely or to consult a knowledgeable attorney to determine potential liability for damages if the lessee were to sustain an "occupational" injury.

3. Setting dates for the completion of a project and inspection of the work done is not formal assurance that the work will be completed satisfactorily. Such an understanding does provide more incentive to plan out the work more thoroughly and to complete it as agreed in the contract. To neglect the deadline and inspection of the work done is equivalent to exposing yourself to the liability of finding a vacated rental unit with a substantial amount of unfinished repair work and perhaps many of the expensive materials missing, also! The thrill of anticipating how something might be changed is entirely different from the actual hour-by-hour effort required to make the desired changes.

MAINTENANCE BEGINS BEFORE YOU BUY

For consistently good results, follow a personal checklist of all relevant maintenance areas which works for you. Learn to anticipate incomplete answers to your direct questions and be persistent-enough to get valid answers to your questions *before* you make that commitment to buy. Don't hesitate to utilize other sources to verify your questions. It is good brinksmanship to have your attorney prepare a legal statement which certifies that the property under consideration has no known defects or deferred maintenance other than what has been described in writing. At the right moment insist that this basically legally binding statement be signed by the seller or the seller's designee. Timing is important in presenting such an "unconventional clause" to a seller since it may obligate the seller to agree to terms other than "seller's fluff" (which is totally unenforcible). It is an excellent clause to have inserted in an earnest money agreement just before you, as the investor, sign. Obvious resistance on the part of the seller at this crucial phase of the negotiation process should immediately be an indication that things are not entirely as they are represented to be. Tactfully hold your ground. Don't be readily bluffed down by pompous sellers and/or their agents who make intimidating remarks such as the following:

1. "That would be most irregular."
2. "Our company [agency] doesn't permit us to make such warranties."
3. "I'm sure you can trust the owner."
4. "I'm sure the seller will tell you anything you want to know about the property. . . . Isn't that right, Mr. Seller?"
5. "That just isn't done!"
6. "You're welcome to inspect the property, but you'll have to accept what the owner says about it [or accept it "as is"]."
7. "This has never been necessary before."
8. "Our company has been in the business for 20 years without ever doing this."

Rental-Property Maintenance 173

As implied above, one of the greatest potential errors you can make as a novice real estate investor is in not accurately assessing the real maintenance needs (deferred, current, and future) and of not making realistic purchase-price adjustments as necessary. A typical investor should be prepared to walk away from nine out of every ten properties he or she researches. The losses in time and money are insignificant compared to the potential obligations and possible losses which can result from committing yourself to an exceptionally poor price, poor terms, or both. One *good* investment every one, two, or three years which approximates your specific goals is all it takes to be a highly successful investor. To do this, an investor must be ultra-sensitive to changing economic conditions, the needs of other people, and be a damned shrewd buyer! The successful investor must critically evaluate all of the factors and make non-emotional decisions on the basis of the numbers. Every seller hopes to find the uncritical buyer who is "ready, willing, and able" to purchase the property as represented and without asking or getting the answers to certain key questions. Most purchasers of residential property buy for need and love—investors must buy "by the numbers" to get a good return on their investment.

The disciplined and the somewhat disciplined investor is basically involved in a race for time against the hypothetically less critical buyer who comes along and assumes that the fair market value is there and submits an offer at a higher price. Sometimes this simply happens. You will likely lose some time and some money in assessing the potential investment and your bid is simply too low or too late. Perhaps you were able to conclude that the price was far too unrealistic to make a profitable return without undo risk. The significant element of knowing as much about the deferred maintenance needs as the seller (ignore for the moment the sales agent who basically only knows what the seller has revealed and what observation cannot deny) is that you may be able to undermine the seller's confidence a little by relating the cost of the deferred maintenance to the current asking price. This can be a dollar-and-cents way to negotiate with any seller whose asking price seems to be the least bit over-inflated. In situations where you may be less certain about the deferred maintenance needs, you can insert protective clauses in the body of the earnest money agreement. Typical clauses such as "in lieu of" an electrical inspection, or "subject to" a plumbing inspection, municipal building inspection, etc., can tie up a property briefly until the specified conditions can be met. Also, competent legal advice on the wording of such conditional clauses can protect you from losing your earnest money deposit and "kill" the offer if desired. Once the conditions have been placed in writing, you should gather your remaining data quickly and thoroughly. Inspections should be conducted by licensed professionals who are employed by you and willing to provide you with a brief, written report of their findings. You will then have a much firmer basis for accepting or rejecting the proposed terms. You will have a tangible instrument in negotiating for better terms with the seller, and you will be acutely aware of maintenance needs which will affect the return on your investment.

THE IMPORTANCE OF CREATIVE LANDSCAPING

Creative landscaping can be favorably compared with creative packaging in the field of marketing. The cost of the materials involved may not be great, but the satisfaction to the purchaser (consumer) is most important. Inattention to the magic of creative landscaping could be a major reason for not attracting the more desirable tenants and, eventually, the eager prospective buyers. The potential consumer (tenant or buyer) is much more likely to take an interest in the interior of a property if he or she is already attracted by the exterior.

Creative landscaping is very much a reflection of good management in general. The natural resources of a given climate, elevation, and geographic location can be enhanced, made clean and "orderly," and contribute significantly to the total value of an investment property. Conversely, property can be neglected, littered with debris, dried up, overgrown, full of weeds, and just plain unattractive or uninteresting. The initial appearance of the property is a very strong non-verbal cue as to the quality of the management and maintenance of the building itself. A well-maintained dwelling may suffer due to unimaginative landscaping. The slightest flaws will be accentuated because of the negative associations that are part of an unfavorable initial impression. A basically well-maintained building with superbly maintained surrounding landscape (and a desirable location) strongly tends to give the appearance of being trouble-free and ultimately results in higher occupancy, higher rents, and higher selling price.

Professional landscaping services can probably be reserved for the larger-income properties in which the owner(s) have little time and/or little interest in planning the landscape design and completing the necessary work themselves. The basic size of an income-producing property will tend to dictate whether professional property managers or landscapers should be involved due to the sheer volume of the area involved. In some situations it may be appropriate to consider a temporary landscape laborer or perhaps of establishing a friendly relationship with the local garden and outdoor nursery where you could be doing a lot of business over the years.

Very basic strategies can be utilized by most of the smaller investors. Minor things such as trimming back bushes, trees, and other greenery can be very important. When prospective tenants or buyers come out to inspect your property, it should not be concealed by vegetation. The ability to see most of the building or buildings from the road makes it easier to maintain some casual surveillance of the property while it is being rented. The increased visibility of the dwelling itself will enhance its significance and make it easier to find. Another strategy is to create a "low-maintenance" landscape when possible and appropriate. Few tenants will voluntarily mow, weed, trim, dethatch, fertilize, and edge a large area of greenery each week when they, like us, have other more pressing things to do with their time.

The single-family dwelling residents can be expected to mow the lawn once or twice each month. Apartment dwellers cannot be expected to assist in any way with landscaping or grounds maintenance. The common solution around multiple-unit dwellings is to landscape extensively with perennials (trees, shrubs, and ground covers) that will do well in your particular climate. Utilize local materials which may be available, such as rock, gravel, barkdust, sawdust, mulch, sand, and related materials. Avoid labor-intensive lawn areas and flowerbeds unless there are no reasonable alternatives. Quality landscaping should blend into the surrounding environment with a minimum of distraction, be attractive, and at least create the illusion of being "low maintenance."

NO PETS ALLOWED

It is the opinion of this writer that the hard-line approach to the subject of pets is the best position to take. It is an inescapable fact that rental properties which allow pets have more difficult maintenance and management problems than units which do not. The list of damages that can be directly traced to a tenant's pet or pets is frequently long and expensive. Dogs and cats especially can be difficult to clean up after because of the odors, stains, hairs, fleas, scratches, and food messes that remain when the tenant moves on. Carpeting, in particular, is often severely damaged or unsalvageable. The prospective tenants with allergies seem to notice any sign of a pet and feel that the unit has not been adequately cleaned. The tenants who are approved to have one pet often seem to acquire additional pets—sometimes a whole litter! Noise, bites, and "droppings" are just part of the potential problems which tend to arise even with conscientious efforts to provide management of the pets. Small puppies sometimes turn into Great Danes! Reptiles and birds can also represent severe management and maintenance problems for the rental owner. When attractive and competitively priced rental units are scarce, prospective tenants will defer the need to have a pet.

SAMPLE CHECKLIST OF THE 12 POTENTIAL MAINTENANCE PROBLEMS

1. Plumbing maintenance: _____
   _____
   _____

2. Electrical maintenance: _____
   _____
   _____

3. Building maintenance: _____
   _____
   _____

4. Heating and air-conditioning maintenance:_____
   _____
   _____

5. Heating and air-conditioning maintenance:_____
   _____
   _____

5. Grounds maintenance and landscaping:_____
   _____
   _____

6. Parking lot maintenance: _____
   _____

7. Garbage and debris maintenance: _____
   _____
   _____

8. Hallway, door, and stairs maintenance: _____
   _____
   _____

9. Laundry room maintenance: _____
   _____
   _____

10. Fire prevention and safety maintenance: _____

11. Appliance maintenance: _____

12. Recreation area (if any) maintenance: _____

10

Creative Ways to Sell or Exchange Income-Producing Properties

The final chapter in the life of an individual income-producing property is typically concluded by one of three different methods—sale, refinance, or exchange.* The variations on these basic themes can be ideally tailored to the individual desires and circumstances of all parties involved in a particular transaction. Investment properties throughout the nation and beyond are being primarily financed by private parties and apart from the prohibitive "conventional" financing of institutional lenders. The "right" structure of a particular transaction will be mostly determined by the economic desirability of the property in question, the seller's complex motivation in marketing the property, and the seller's various tax consequences under one of the three basic methods. Each transaction will be further complicated by the necessity of negotiation between parties with essentially opposing interests. There's the necessity of reaching a "meeting of the minds" to successfully cope with the complexities of single and/or multiple transactions in a timely and mutually satisfactory manner. The three basic methods for the disposition of income-producing property are as follows:

---

*Rare forms of disposition of real property might include "gift," devise through a will (probate), fire loss, abandonment, governmental confiscation (I.R.S.), condemnation, default-bankruptcy, and so on.

1. Direct or Installment Sale
2. Refinance
3. Exchange

DIRECT OR INSTALLMENT SALE

The question in the seller's mind about considering either a direct sale or an installment sale should be readily answerable in terms of: (a) the adjusted sale price equity; (b) what the proceeds of the sale are to be used for; and (c) the seller's tax consequences. The decision should *not* be left to the buyer's preferences. Relatively precise information should be obtained from your personal C.P.A. or tax consultant before seriously involving yourself with your personal real estate broker, or with potential buyers. The basic distinctions between the two categories are relatively easy to apply. Any sale in which *more* than 30% of the total sale price (including all down payment monies and principle payments) is received during the year of sale, the total net proceeds of the sale will be taxed as if the *total* amount of the sale had been received during the year of sale. Obviously, this Internal Revenue Service "30-Percent Rule"* can severely penalize the unwary seller. Suppose, for example, that an individual sells an income-producing property for $100,000 and the taxable net profit was an even $40,000. By accepting $31,000 in down payment *and* principle payments in the year of sale, the seller must pay the capital gains taxes *as if* the full $40,000 had been received ($40,000 × .40 capital gains × .45 tax bracket = $7,200 due in taxes). If that same party accepted a gross total of $26,000 in the year of sale, only that amount of money would be taxed in that year ($26,000 × .40 capital gains × .45 tax bracket = $4,680 due in taxes). The distinctions are that although the direct-sale method brought in an additional $5,000, the direct-sale method cost an additional $2,520 in taxes that year (which could have been deferred and utilized), for a net gain of only $2,480, *and* the

---

*See "Tax Reform Act of 1976." Information available at local Internal Revenue Service offices.

possibility of being pushed into a higher overall tax bracket. One of the most important distinctions between a direct sale and an installment sale for most sellers is that a given property is far more likely to be marketed quickly and with the best possible terms under the installment sale. With this method the seller can accept a total of approximately 20% to 28% of the sale price in the first year. This lower down payment requirement will obviously attract more buyers and better terms than the 30% to 50% (and above) requirement that must be invested to "cash out" the typical seller's sale price equity. Most investors want to exercise the maximum benefits of leverage and obtain the best possible tax position relative to the amount of money to be invested. Therefore, *most* investors will seek reliable income-producing properties in which the sellers ultimately demand no more than 20% to 28% of the actual sale price as a down payment and year-of-sale principle payment. There are relatively few investors who will willingly tie up their dollars by making 35% to 50% down payments even though 35% to 50% is the typical *least* amount of equity that the seller will possess at the time of sale. The bind that sellers often get into is in wanting to acquire an even larger investment property which is approximately 75% larger than the current sale-price equity they have to work with. A secondary issue for the seller is: "Why should I accept a fairly large contract back at 10% to 12% annual interest when I know from experience that I can make from 35% to 50% per year (and more) by investing my money in suitable income-producing properties?" These are just two of the frequently opposing questions which must be resolved in the negotiation process between the buyer and seller. Related buyer-seller questions could be: "How tight do I make the balloon payment at the end of the contract? Two years? Five years? Longer? Do I make the payoff subject to available refinance monies? What amount of liquidated damages should there be each month for failure to meet the deadline?" A separate question for the seller could well be: "How urgent might it be for me to convert the contract to cash at a discount?" The basic rule of thumb is that unseasoned (less than one year old) contracts typically suffer approximately a 25% discount when it becomes necessary to "dump" them on the mortgage paper market. Contracts which are "seasoned"—that is, where payments have reliably been made for one year or longer (and equities increased)—typically suffer only a 10% discount on the mortgage paper or contract paper markets. Matured contracts can often be traded at face value for other investment property when they are well secured and show a good monthly yield. The seller, then, must decide if he or she can afford to hold a contract for at least 12 months. Also, will it be possible to arrange financing now or at a future date to have the contract accepted as a portion of a future down payment without suffering a discount? Did the sale price fully allow for a 10% to 25% possible discount *before* the contract was accepted? Was the contract made up by the seller's personal attorney who is experienced in drafting legally binding land sales contracts? Are the terms of the contract "definite and certain"? Does the contract specify sufficient controls over late payments, property management, insurance coverage, title insurance, liquidated damages, and a sufficient annual interest rate to produce an acceptable yield for a possible contract buyer?

REFINANCE

The pervasive effects of inflation throughout the economy have made the option of refinancing an existing income-producing property a more likely option. By maintaining control of the properties that an investor is already in possession of, the investor continues to take advantage of the single-most important asset of income-producing properties in an inflationary economy—appreciation. Another tangible explanation of the investor's increased motivation to refinance existing properties is that there are no taxes on borrowed money. Unless too expensive to be reasonably obtained, refinance monies will ordinarily be available at a basically known rate of interest—especially from private sources. Also, there are usually no specific limitations on how that well-secured, borrowed money may be used. The investor with a high-equity property can elect to retain possession of a desirable income property and any benefits that may be associated with that property. The favorable cash flow from such a property will easily offset the deductible interest rate that must be paid on the refinanced money. This restructuring of a high-equity property will not improve the amount of depreciation that can be taken on that property, but it does allow the investor to create additional sources for depreciation through the acquisition of additional income-producing properties. These newly acquired investment properties will also provide a much greater annual return than the cost of the refinanced money. The risks of excessive "over-financing" of multiple income-producing properties are self evident. In conservatively refinancing a high-equity property, the minimal risks are simply that the debt service (monthly loan and/or mortgage payments) on the original and the newly acquired income-producing property is increased over what would be the case if only traditional forms of financing were applied. The most important advantage of arranging for such financing is that the investor can now benefit from the *appreciation* on two or more income-producing properties. Another distinct advantage is that a tax event has not been triggered on the refinanced property and the suddenly higher debt service prevents the high-equity property from creating big tax problems when it otherwise showed a higher and higher annual cash flow. An incidental advantage is that the interest paid on the refinanced money is fully deductible from the investor's personal income tax whether or not the money is used for additional investments. In a "buyer's market" it can make sense to refinance a high-equity property up to 80% of the appraised value and then promptly sell the property directly with a required down payment of perhaps 20% to 25%, or less! However, the basic rationale for refinancing and immediately acquiring additional income-producing property is that the investor can now seek appropriate, highly leveraged investment properties by using these tax-exempt dollars as the basis of the new down payment. The risk in over-utilizing this procedure, as suggested above, is that in applying this method of "100% financing" of a new investment property, the investor could become "over-financed" during a period of extended economic setbacks (such as a severe local recession) and could be *obligated* to sell some holdings to keep this "financial empire" intact. A common technique is to refinance enough money to minimize the tax consequences of too much positive cash flow with a high-equity property and to conservatively acquire an additional property (using additional unborrowed and/or partnership funds) that will likely support the high debt service of perhaps 80%, 90%, or even 95% financing. This method of financing can be especially productive for the individual or individuals who are forced into high personal income tax brackets because of high average earnings or other taxable income and someone who may welcome the appropriate "small alligator."

SAMPLE REFINANCING PROCEDURE

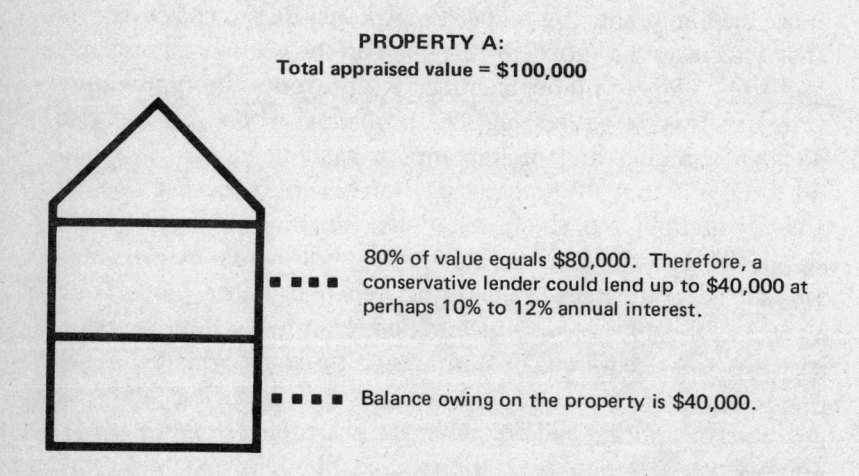

PROPERTY A:
Total appraised value = $100,000

■ ■ ■ ■ 80% of value equals $80,000. Therefore, a conservative lender could lend up to $40,000 at perhaps 10% to 12% annual interest.

■ ■ ■ ■ Balance owing on the property is $40,000.

PROPERTY B:
Total value of $250,000
and is to be acquired with mostly refinanced monies.

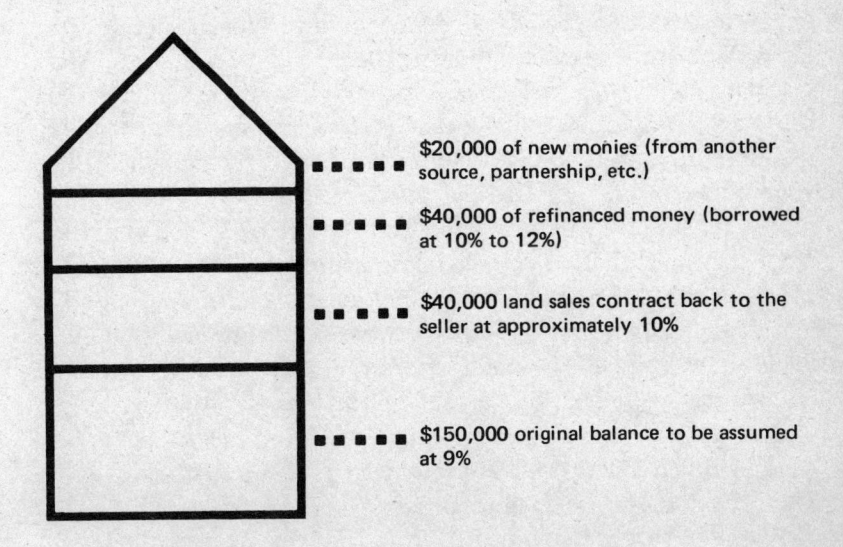

$20,000 of new monies (from another source, partnership, etc.)

$40,000 of refinanced money (borrowed at 10% to 12%)

$40,000 land sales contract back to the seller at approximately 10%

$150,000 original balance to be assumed at 9%

The same investor now controls both properties ($350,000 in value) with a "real" equity of $60,000, or 17% of the total valuation!

TAX-DEFERRED EXCHANGES

A great deal of razzle-dazzle has been associated with the idea of exchanging real property to defer (not evade) capital gains taxes. The assumed advantages of capital gains tax deferral on investment properties often obscure the pressure upon the parties of the exchange to agree upon estimated mutual equities that are the essential trading stock. Oftentimes these assumed equities must be agreed to without being "tested" on the open competitive market. Also, there is the obligation to absorb the multiple real estate commissions that are routinely incorporated as part of each exchanger's overall cost. The individual who is trading up pays a negotiated commission and absorbs the higher cost which is necessitated by the real estate commission on the property to be acquired. The individual trading down experiences a capital gains tax event on the adjusted sales profit (after deducting the allowable basis and after adjusting the sale price to allow for the standard commission). The basic pattern remains essentially the same irregardless of the number of transactions that are tied together in "a single deal." Your established relationship with your personal broker, personal attorney, and personal certified public accountant will be indispensable in providing you with the necessary consultation prior to committing yourself to unfavorable exchange terms because of the "magic" of deferred capital gains taxes. With the assistance of these professionals, you can decide for yourself whether or not a particular set of circumstances will result in a personally desirable exchange.

The tax-deferred property exchange is an excellent tool to be used with creativity and discretion by real-property investors. The effectiveness and appropriateness of a tax-deferred exchange will vary with time and circumstances. This method will "fit" some investors far more advantageously than it will others. A slow, methodical series of well-planned exchanges could be ideal for the mature investor who wants to build the maximum possible estate and defer the capital gains taxes until a lower tax bracket can be attained in the future. An exchange upward can be ideal for the individual who has allowed equities to disproportionately build up and who would otherwise trigger a severe tax event that would limit the dollars available for a newly structured investment. Another individual who wants to convert investment property to cash could structure a three-way exchange in which the property accepted in exchange would be lawfully pre-sold to a third party. Exchanges can be prepared involving "like kind" investments between different cities, different types of investment property (residential *vs.* commercial, industrial *vs.* farm, etc.), and be expanded to ultimately meet the basic needs of each party in the transaction. If the various individual needs of one investor could not be met, the exchange either would not happen, or another investor might be quickly substituted into the transaction to make everything work. Once this method of tax deferral is utilized, it is difficult to avoid dependency upon future exchanges because of the *low basis* that is successively transferred each time. The young investor with limited amounts of equity for trading stock and/or the agressive investor who turns properties over every year or two and who works with thin equities will tend to not gain appreciably from the mechanics of the tax-deferred exchange.

In addition to "solving investment problems" that might not be solved in any other manner, the principle advantage of exchanging an investment property for a "like kind" investment property of greater value is that all capital gains taxes are deferred, but not forgiven. Thus, by applying the principle of *leverage,* these temporarily exempted tax dollars can also be used to acquire three, four, or even five dollars toward the next investment property for each tax-deferred dollar. This method (also known as "pyramiding") can provide the individual or group investor with additional purchasing power to more rapidly move up the investment scale in terms of valuation and therefore in terms of increased tax shelter to ultimately ease the burden of those cumulative capital gains taxes that are linked to each consecutive exchange.

The basic concept of investment property exchange is relatively simple. The legal authorization for exchanging, Internal Revenue Service Section 1031, has been around for years. It is the details and all of the variable combinations in exchanging that can become complex and/or confusing. The 1979 edition of the "Internal Revenue Service Publication 544" briefly states that: "Gain from certain exchanges of property is not taxed, nor is loss deductible, at the time of the exchange. The new property is treated as being substantially a continuation of the old unliquidated investment. Taxation of the gain or deduction of the loss on such an exchange is postponed until you dispose of the property received in the exchange. In the case of a corporate reorganization, the new enterprise or new corporate structure is treated substantially as a continuation of the old."* The five basic criteria of a "nontaxable exchange" are:

1. "There must be a reciprocal transfer." A "like kind" business or investment property must be exchanged for another. It is not sufficient to exchange an investment property wholly for cash. If something of value is exchanged in addition to a "like kind" property (also known as "boot"), the fair-market value of that something becomes taxable as a capital gain.
2. "A loss is never recognized." The loss is computed as a portion of the adjusted basis and is economically balanced out at the time when the non-taxable exchange is converted to a taxable event.
3. "Exchange of property for like property." This refers to the demonstrated intent in holding either undeveloped land, business property, or income-producing property. The intent had to be for investment purposes and/or income production, not simply personal use. Any of the following types of investments could be non-taxably exchanged when all five criteria are met: vacant land, rental houses, business properties, apartment houses, commercial buildings, industrial properties, office buildings, shopping centers, and related.
4. "Must not be property held for sale." A "dealer" or sales agent cannot qualify for a non-taxable exchange of properties which are merely held for resale to customers. It must be demonstrated that the properties to be exchanged were actually used for either business or investment purposes. The most commonly excluded properties would be those held as a personal residence; properties which do not qualify for capital gains treatment, or those properties which are to be offered for sale immediately after the non-taxable exchange.
5. "Must be business or investment property." This is merely a reiteration of items #3 and #4 above that the property must qualify for capital gains treatment to be eligible for consideration as a non-taxable exchange.**

---

*"Internal Revenue Service Publication 544," 1979 edition, p. 3.
**Ibid., p. 3.

EXCHANGE EXAMPLE A

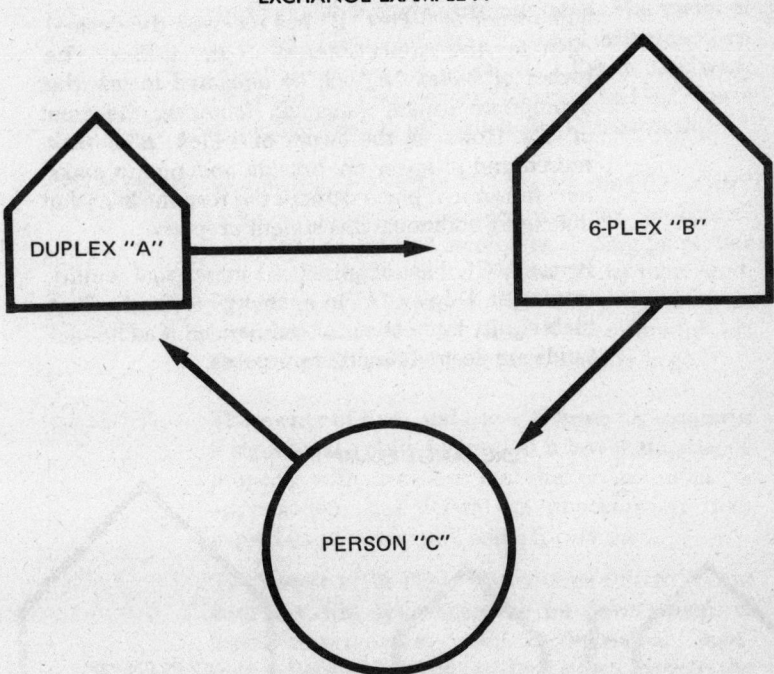

```
    DUPLEX "A"  ──────►  6-PLEX "B"
                              │
                              ▼
                         PERSON "C"
```

PROBLEM: The owner of 6-Plex "B" wants to convert the investment property to cash, and, since this individual is retiring, a duplex is *not* wanted.

SOLUTION: The owner of Duplex "A" is intent upon acquiring 6-Plex "B" as a non-taxable (deferred capital gains tax) exchange upward. The solution is to carefully structure the sale of the duplex to Person "C" in such a manner that upon closing, *all* of the cashed-out equity in Duplex "A" goes directly to the owner of 6-Plex-"B."

RESULT: The owner of Duplex "A" exchanges every bit of the accumulated sale price equity into the desired

The owner of 8-Plex "A" wants the full advantages of income-property ownership without the sporadic demands of residential-property management. The solution was to exchange for a commercial property with a long-term, net, net lease and far less management responsibility. Both properties had existing mortgages which essentially canceled each other out. The figures were approximately as follows:

PROPERTY "A" PROPERTY "B"

EQUALIZATION OF EQUITIES

	PROPERTY "A"		PROPERTY "B"
FMV	$200,000	FMV	$180,000
Basis	110,000	Basis	145,000
Balance	85,000	Balance	110,000
Equity	115,000	Equity	70,000
Equalizer	-0-	Equalizer	45,000
Balance	115,000	Balance	115,000

REDISTRIBUTION OF BASIS

	PROPERTY "A"		PROPERTY "B"
Sale price	$200,000	Sale price	$180,000
Minus old basis	110,000	Minus old basis	145,000
Recognized gain	+90,000	Recognized gain	+35,000
Minus cash rec'd.	−45,000	Minus cash rec'd.	-0-
Basis of property conveyed	+110,000	Basis of property conveyed	+145,000
Mortgage assumed	+110,000	Mortgage assumed	+85,000
Mortgage canceled	−85,000	Mortgage canceled	−110,000
New basis =	$180,000	New basis =	$155,000

SELECTING YOUR PERSONAL REAL ESTATE BROKER

A good general rule is to *never* select a real estate broker or a sales representative at random. The variability among real estate personnel, like all professions, can range from the totally incompetent to the totally indispensable representative. Investors simply must be more selective and independently knowledgeable than the occasional buyer and seller of real estate. *Most* licensed real estate agents (and even most brokers) can be considered too inexperienced to effectively represent income-property investors. Constructive action must actually be taken to differentiate between the inappropriate residential sales agent and the highly competent, professional broker who possesses a successful background in working with income-producing properties. The "typical" real estate sales representative is predominantly trained and/or experienced in listing and selling owner-occupied dwellings to basically naïve clients who are unfamiliar with anything except "conventional" financing. Such experience will be of little value to the creative and resourceful income-property investor.

An investor cannot afford to wait until he or she is ready to either buy or sell to select the right broker. Care should be taken well in advance to establish a personal and philosophical relationship between yourself and the broker of choice *before* the task of either selling or buying an income-producing property is to be accomplished. Of necessity, the highly ambitious and/or assertive investor will often become sufficiently knowledgeable in the various aspects of income-producing properties to comfortably acquire, manage, and creatively dispose of investment properties without a broker. However, since a broker will quite often be involved, it's important to know that the person is actually "in *your* corner." It's worthwhile to take some extra precautions to be certain that the broker of choice will be contractually representing and working for *you*, not the other person! Verbal understandings alone can often turn to misunderstandings and the appearance of misrepresentations. That polite, friendly, and conscientious representative of a well-established real estate office may be strictly representing the other party. In fact, to attempt to equally represent the best interests of both parties (seller and buyer) is actually a legal violation of the fiduciary relationship. Therefore, as a serious investor it is unjustifiable to gamble with your time and money by allowing yourself to be "sweet-talked" into a contractual relationship by some unknown, "silver-tongued" realtor. The after-the-fact frustrations and the potential financial losses can be staggering.

The basic test in selecting the "right" personal broker is to make inquiries of the local board of realtors, home-owner's associations, apartment-owner's associations, other investors, allied vendors, lending institutions, and/or other professional groups. Obtain the suggested names of at least three or four *brokers* who are known to have an interest and successful experience in the general type of investment property that *you* want to work with. The next step is to personally meet with several of these suggested brokers. Are you highly compatible with this other person? Can you arrange for repeated opportunities to discuss some specific concerns? Can you establish a good basis for acquaintance without being "just another investor" to that broker, or without being sold what that broker *has*, rather than what you *want*? Now, if the "chemistry" between yourself and the broker of choice is a positive one, consciously work to build and preserve that relationship. Consciously work to familiarize the broker of choice with your personal capabilities, aspirations, resources, and so on. This should be done, of course, after you have independently determined that the broker of choice is an established, reputable, and genuinely knowledgeable individual. The basically simple criterion for attempting to verify all of these "virtues" is to verify that the broker of choice is a member (and an *active* member) of the local board of realtors and other professional associations. Is the broker of choice active in other community affairs? The well-established and well-maintained relationship with an appropriate broker of choice can pay very big dividends for yourself and the broker. Don't begrudge the occasional commissions that must be paid. Keep that broker working for you. The well-established relationship with a personal broker will assist you tremendously in remaining up to date with the tempo of the local investment market, the unusual opportunities that sporadically occur, and the potential danger spots or unexpectedly high-risk investment properties that you might otherwise stumble into.

The same basic strategy can and should be applied in acquiring and maintaining a working relationship with the other professionals on your *team*. The most important members of that team will be your personal certified public accountant, personal attorney, institutional lender, insurance agent, and perhaps other support personnel "of choice." As the *team* develops, these individuals can be relied upon more and more in assisting you with the data necessary to make critical decisions about the rapidly changing elements of income-producing property investments. Their assistance in helping you with error reduction will directly contribute to your attainment of personal investment goals and a highly profitable experience for all. Quietly and with perhaps little change in your present career and/or life-style, it will be *you* as the income-property investor who will receive the greatest return. Less than 5% of the adult population is out there actually doing it! You can be part of that 5%. You can start developing your *team* right now if you have not already done so. You can attain the promise of this instructional text of "doubling your investment every two to three years with income-producing properties!" The next step is "out there." The rewards for honest and diligent efforts are certain to exceed your greatest expectations. Income-producing property is the only reliable "investment vehicle" with a strong enough performance record for novice and expert alike to double their initial investment *every* two to three years!

Glossary

Abstract of Title: a chronological history of the title to land; a condensed summary of all recorded claims, liens, encumbrances, and titles to a particular piece of land; obtained to prove the title is clear and the owner has the legal right to sell the property

Acceleration Clause: generally a clause in a mortgage which entitles the lender to demand immediate payment in full upon the occurrence of a specified event—*e.g.*, 60-day delinquency of payments, sale of property

Acceptance: the act of accepting (usually by signature) an offer which results in a binding contract. In real estate it is often the act of the seller or his agent in agreeing to the terms of the agreement of sale and approval of the negotiations through acknowledgment & acceptance of the deposit monies or promissory note.

Access Right: the right of an owner to enter and exit from his property. When he must cross the land of another, this is generally referred to as an easement.

Acknowledgment: a sworn statement made before a notary public; generally applies to statements signed before a notary public, or any signature on a binding contract which is the "evidence" of an acceptance

Acquisition: the process or act by which a person obtains property

Acre: a measure of land which equals 43,560 square feet, 4,840 square yards, 160 rods, or 4,047 square meters

Administrator: an individual appointed by the probate court to administer the total estate of a deceased person who died intestate—*i.e.*, one who left no will

Ad Valorem: according to value—*e.g.*, a property tax which is levied according to the value of the property

Affidavit: a written statement which is signed and sworn to before authorized witnesses, or a notary public

Agreement of Sale: an enforcible, written contract between seller and purchaser in which agreement is reached in the terms and conditions of the sale of real property

Alienation: the actual transfer of real property from one person to another; the transference of possession from one person to another

Allocation: the determination of the relative value of land, improvements, and personal property for the purposes of computing depreciation

Amenity: one or more pleasant or desirable qualities which increase the value of real estate to the owner (seller or purchaser)

Amortization: the gradual reduction of a loan through regular installment payments. Basically, the term refers to the principle, interest, taxes, and insurance (P.I.T.I) payments throughout the life of the loan and to the point of extinction of the indebtedness.

Annuity: a sum of money or its equivalent which is received as part of a formal schedule of payments (usually paid quarterly or annually)

Appraisal: a casual to technical estimate and opinion of value at a certain point in time. Numerous methods are generally used to obtain a creditable appraisal (*cf.* capitalization method, comparable sales, summation, replacement cost).

Appreciation: increase in value due to upgrading, inflation, good location, favorable supply-and-demand ratios, and other complex economic factors; optimistically figured into most future earnings projections

Appurtenance: those rights or items of value which transfer incidentally with the transfer of ownership—*i.e.*, timber rights, easements, right of way, garage, tool shed, etc.

Assessed value: the value placed upon real property by the local government for tax purposes and within statutory guidelines. Generally the assessment is a percentage of the estimated true value (*e.g.*, 100%).

Assumption: the act of assuming the mortgage indebtedness of another, and, in addition, of purchasing the former mortgagee's equity

Attachment: the act of impounding or seizing property by court order to settle past-due debts

Balloon Payment: a formal contract in which the final payment is greater than the regular payment and upon which the balance is paid in full

Bargain and Sale Deed: a deed which conveys real property in exchange for valuable consideration; generally involves an escrow arrangement

Basis: Essentially, basis is the original cost of acquisition of real property plus the cost of added improvements made by the seller and minus the depreciation already claimed by the seller. In other words, the economic "basis" is that amount of an investment property which is exempt from taxation at the time of sale, or exchange.

Bench Marks: any durable marker used by surveyors to locate or establish formal boundaries

Betterment: a municipal improvement which increases the value of real property—*e.g.*, paved roads, curbs, sidewalks, streetlights, sewers, etc.

Bilateral Contract: any contract in which both parties expressly enter into reciprocal agreements

Bill of Sale: a formal written document which transfers title to real property to the purchaser

Binder: a written agreement to cover part or all of the down payment on real property as evidence of good faith on the part of the purchaser (*cf.* Earnest Money Agreement); also, a form utilized by insurance men to assure lenders that a transferred parcel of property will be insured

Blanket Mortgage: a single mortgage on two or more parcels of real property and used generally as security on a single loan

Blighted Area: any area which is currently (or formerly) declining in economic value due to negative economic factors, such as neglected or abandoned buildings, conspicuously inadequate building maintenance, chaotic zoning regulations, overcrowding, economic obsolescence, and rapidly depreciating buildings

Breach: violation of the law; failure to perform a contractual obligation, either by omission or commission

Broker: a formally licensed or certified individual who is employed on a commission basis by one principle only and to facilitate the legal transfer of interests in real estate (*cf.* Fiduciary Relationship)

Building Code: the regulation of the construction of buildings within a particular municipality by ordinance and/or law

Bundle of Rights: analogous to a bundle of sticks in which each stick represents a separate right or privilege. Therefore, the ownership of real property entails a bundle or rights, such as the right to use, lease, will, sell, give away, privacy, make improvements or changes, and to control the use of such within the scope of the law.

Capitalization: the process of converting annual net income into an estimate of current fair market value (F.M.V.). The net income is divided by the capitalization rate to give a percentage figure of the anticipated return on the investment.

Capitalization Rate (CAP Rate): the percentage figure used to evaluate the approximate total price of an investment property. To determine CAP rate, divide the Net Operating Income (*i.e.*, gross income minus vacancies and expenses equals N.O.I.) by the asking price.

Cash Flow: Cash flow is an accounting term which refers to the actual surplus or spendable dollars remaining in an investment property after all expenses have been met (*e.g.*, mortgage, taxes, expenses, vacancies, depreciation, etc.). A positive cash flow is a part of the profit to be derived from investment property. A negative cash flow means total expenses exceed total income and additional monies must come out of pocket to maintain the investment.

Caveat Emptor: a warning to all buyers. Literally, this Latin phrase may be interpreted as: "Let the Buyer Beware." This is a prominent concern with respect to real estate due to the multiplicity of known and unknown factors involved, potential for misrepresentation, and the economic vagaries of the future (*i.e.*, risk *vs.* security).

Chattel: any personal property, as distinguished from real property

Chattel Mortgage: the use of personal property as a security for the performance of an act or payment of an obligation

Cloud on the Title: any encumbrance or unsettled claim which, if proven valid in court, would affect or impair the issuance of a clear title, or the ability to lawfully purchase or sell real property. This is the usual rationale for requiring a title search.

Common Law: a body of law which originated in England through custom and practice. In most instances this body of law has been superceded by statutory law (*cf.* common law and community property states).

Community Property: All property which is acquired or accumulated by husband and wife living together is considered to be through their joint efforts and therefore shared equally.

Comparable Sales: a method of appraising property values by establishing one or more normative properties or models which are closely matched for size, location, similarity of construction, number of rooms, amenities, age, etc. This method typically renders a value or construction cost per square foot; for example, a 1,000-square-foot apartment unit which is found to be valued at $26 per square foot would be a useful norm for comparing similar investment properties.

Concurrent Ownership: when title to a particular parcel of real estate is held by two or more unrelated persons at the same time (compare common property, joint tenancy, tenancy in common, and community property)

Condemnation: the legal process of converting privately held real property to public use by a governmental body. In all instances, just consideration, or fair market value, must be paid. It is also known as the right of eminent domain.

Condominium: a multiple-unit dwelling in which a resident or nonresident purchaser could ultimately acquire a fee-simple ownership of the living unit and joint ownership of the common areas of the structure and the land. Regular fees are assessed for management and maintenance expenses (sometimes described as a vertical subdivision). "Recreational" condominiums are typically not recommended as investment properties.

Contract: a legally enforceable agreement between two or more parties that is generally in writing (occasionally oral) which stipulates the terms and conditions under which the obligated parties will either perform or refrain from performing some task in accordance with the express wishes of the initiating party, and in exchange for some consideration. Contracts are either valid, unenforceable, void, or voidable. All contracts pertaining to the sale of real property must be in writing (cf. Statute of Frauds).

Contract of Sale: a written contract in which the purchaser and the seller agree to terms and conditions for the sale and conveyance of real estate (cf. Land Sales Contract, Contract to Purchase Real Estate, Conditional Sales Contract)

Conveyance: the transfer of the title (deed) in real property from one to another; usually from the seller to the purchaser

Cooperative: a multiple-unit dwelling in which the title to the building and land is held entirely by a corporation or trust and in which each tenant-owner holds a portion of the stock in the corporation. The cost of the stock will vary with the value of the total investment.

Covenant: agreements written into deeds or mortgages which promise specific action or inaction or specific uses or non-uses of a particular property.

Cul-De-Sac: a dead-end street. Often such a street will have a circular turnaround at the closed end.

Deed: a written legal document used in the official transfer of real estate ownership. To meet all requirements it must be properly executed, acknowledged, and delivered to the purchaser (grantee).

Defeasance: a legally recognized condition which, when fulfilled, has the effect of nullifying some other condition in the deed or mortgage

Depreciation: basically a decline in value of any resource held for investment purposes. The decline may be brought about by aging, physical deterioration, functional or economic obsolescence, or other causes. As recognized by the I.R.S., depreciation is an investment incentive which is legally authorized by law and operates as an allowable tax deducation against the income of an asset.

Devise: a gift of real estate by last will and testament

Discrimination: in real estate, any prejudice or differential treatment in the willingness to rent or sell to a person because of sex, race, religion, or assumed ethnic background

Domicile: one's permanent home; the residence to which a person customarily returns after being away; usually identified as one's immediate home or permanent address

Earnest Money Agreement: generally a signed agreement with a token (sometimes the entire down payment or a fraction thereof) payment made as evidence of genuine intent to proceed in the purchase of real estate. Depending upon how the earnest money agreement is written, it is questionable whether it is a legally binding contract or merely an offer to buy. Traditionally, it is more enforceable by the buyer than the seller.

Easement: the right of ingress and egress across another's property. An easement is generally created by necessity and is established by written agreement or long-term usage. It is the right, privilege, or interest which one person has in the land of another. It is an encumbrance against the property which is subject to it.

Economic Life: the estimated number of years which an investment property can be expected to yield a profitable return. First-owner properties are typically figured at 40 years' economic life. Older properties are likely to be determined at somewhat shorter times.

Encroachment: any physical object, such as a wall, fence, eaves, overhang, etc., which extends onto the property of another

Encumbrance: any claim, lien, charge, or liability which affects or limits the fee-simple title to real property—*e.g.*, unpaid taxes, deficiency judgment, right of way, or easement

Equity: the economic interest or value which the purchaser acquires in real property above all other indebtedness, such as the mortgage; also described as the reduction of a mortgage or contractual indebtedness

Equity of Redemption: the original owner's right to redeem property within a prescribed period of time after a foreclosure action results in the sale of the property. The redemption must include payment of all debts, interest, and costs to date.

Escalator Clause: a distinct clause in a contract which permits upward or downward adjustment of certain items in the event of formally described contingencies

Escheat: When there are no known heirs, the estate of a deceased person reverts to the state.

Escrow: use of a neutral third party to carry out the provisions of a contractual agreement, including financial arrangements, until the agreement between two or more persons is complete

Estate: the quantity, nature, degree, and extent of interest which a person has in certain real property; a legal interest or right in property.

Exchange: a reciprocal transfer of investment properties. Real estate which is used for investment purposes may be exchanged for other investment real estate of equal or greater value without an immediate tax obligation for any gain or loss on the transaction (see Section 1031 of the Internal Revenue Code). Taxes are merely deferred, not exempted. In exchanging downward, there is a tax obligation in the year of the transaction.

Fee Simple Absolute: the most complete level of real estate ownership—that is, free of all financial conditions and limitations; freely assignable to devises, free to sell, lease, rent, etc., within the limits of the law; also referred to as fee simple, or, more briefly, as fee or freehold.

Fiduciary Relationship: a person in a position of trust and confidence, such as between a principle and his agent. The broker has a legal duty to represent the best interests of his principle—the seller, or the buyer, but not both simultaneously. Brokers and agents typically represent the seller, *not* the buyer.

Fixture: any article which was originally personal property and has since become attached to the real property in such a way as to become an inseparable part of the real property, thus passing with the sale.

Functional Depreciation: decline in value due to inadequate changes or omissions—*e.g.*, the absence of a closet or storage space; one bathroom in a four-bedroom house; missing doors; absence of a second exit, etc.

G.I. Loan: a mortgage loan which is guaranteed by the Veterans Administration and available only to honorably discharged veterans and their widows (if they remain unmarried prior to use)

Gift Deed: a deed in which the consideration is "love and affection." No other material consideration is required. This is rare, obviously.

Graduated Lease: a lease which provides for a variable rental rate; a typically long-term lease. Rent may be determined by the gross income of the property (*cf.* Percentage Lease), or rent assessments may be based on periodic appraisals.

Grantee: a person to whom real property is transferred or conveyed—*i.e.*, the buyer

Grantor: a person who conveys real property by deed—*i.e.*, the seller

Gross Income: the total income from an investment property, including all rents, deposits, and other sources of income connected with the property, and prior to deductions for expenses, mortgage, etc.

Gross Lease: a lease of real property in which the lessor is required to pay all property expenses as though he were the owner of the property

Gross Profit: the surplus or profit after sale between the total received and the total paid for the property. Gross profit is computed before deductions for all indebtedness, selling expenses, depreciation, etc.

Gross Rent Multiplier: a method of determining an estimate of value. The gross income is multiplied by a factor which is locally established as a good approximation of value for different kinds of investment properties and in different locations—*e.g.*, "5.7 x gross" with a gross income of $9,500 equals $52,350. This last figure would be the approximate selling price of the investment property.

Habendum Clause: a distinct clause in a deed in which the principle of private ownership of property is affirmed; also known as the "to have and hold" clause

Hereditaments: any property—whether real, personal, corporeal, or incorporeal—which may be inherited

Highest and Best Use: an appraisal concept in describing real property which means the current use which is most likely to produce the greatest overall return over a given period of time. The concept is applied most often when property is in a state of transition.

Holdover Tenant: any tenant who remains in possession of leased property after the expiration of the lease

Homestead: real estate which is protected against judgments up to a certain valuation. To qualify, the homestead rights must be properly recorded in the deed, and the property must be used as the primary residence of the owner.

Hypothecate: the act of offering something as security without the necessity of actually relinquishing possession of it; typically applies to one who refinances existing resources with the intent of acquiring additional investment properties

Improvements: any addition to raw land which tends to enhance its value—*e.g.*, buildings, streets, sewers, etc. In computing depreciation, improvements reflect the value of the structure as distinguished from the value of the land (no depreciation) and the personal property (a more accelerated rate of depreciation).

Income Approach: one of a number of appraisal methods used in determining the approximate value of an income-producing property. The assumption is that the value of the property is the total worth of the net income it will produce during the remainder of its productive life.

Incurable Depreciation: a structural defect of significant proportions which would be financially impractical or impossible to correct

Installment Contract: purchase of real estate with the installment method. Upon default, payments are forfeited (*cf.* Land Contract).

Investment: that medium which produces a reasonably safe return, sooner or later. An investment can also be described as an asset which has the potential or capability to produce a profit. The four primary elements of an investment are risk, quantity of income, quality of income, and length of term (time parameters).

Joint Tenancy: the holding of real estate by two or more persons who share equally in the ownership and use of the property and with the right to survivorship to the other grantees

Land Contract: a contract for the purchase of real estate on the installment basis. Typically, the seller agrees to convey title when a predetermined amount has been paid or when the price is paid in full. The disadvantages is that the seller can reclaim the property in a default. One of the advantages is that the property can often be purchased with a low down payment (high leverage) and lower-than-average interest rates (*cf.* Land Sales Contract, Installment Contract).

Landlord: an archaic term which has survived from the feudal era, when a "lord," or the nobility, held possession of all of the land in the name of the king. In return for allowing the serf (tenant) to farm the land, the serf gave the lord a portion of the crop and his military support in the event of a war. Literally, the term now refers to anyone who rents land to another (replaced somewhat by terms such as "manager," or "professional manager").

Lease: generally a written rental agreement (Louisiana is the primary exception) between the owner of real estate and the tenant who seeks occupancy in exchange for reasonable consideration. A typical lease would specify the terms, conditions, duration, rental amounts, other charges, and expiration dates to be applied to a specific property.

Leasehold: the contractual authority to occupy and/or use for business purposes a property which is owned by another. For example, under a leasehold an investor could lawfully operate an office building just as if the building were his own during the life-span of the lease. As far as the tenants are concerned, the investor would, in fact, be the landlord. The investor's equity in the building vanishes when the leasehold expires.

Leverage: essentially refers to the use of large sums of other people's money (O.P.M.) to control an investment. Real estate investments of virtually any size can often be controlled with no more than a 10% to 20% interest. Some investments in real estate are controlled with 100% leverage.

Lien: a legal claim by one or more persons against the real property or other tangible assets of another as security for the payment of a debt or discharge of an obligation (*cf.* mortgages, judgments, taxes).

Limited Partnership: Although the definition varies slightly from state to state, the general meaning is that there can be a number of limited partners in addition to the general partners who have a limited liability—*i.e.*, at most, they cannot lose more than their total assets which they have already invested. In a general partnership, if the assets prove insufficient in a bankruptcy suit, the creditors can make claims upon all other assets in addition which the partners may hold.

Liquidity: the ability to quickly convert an asset into cash without a penalty. Few things do not suffer a discount when urgently dumped upon the market. On the average, real estate has traditionally had a low level of liquidity due to the size and complexity of the investment. Real estate is a significant hedge against inflation; it is rarely sold at a loss when it is well managed. Profit-taking is just one of the factors which contributes to the low liquidity.

Market Value: the highest price which a buyer would voluntarily pay, and the lowest price which a seller would voluntarily accept. Market Value, or Fair Market Value (F.M.V.) also implies reasonableness in exposure to the market—*i.e.*, reasonable time, reasonable knowledge of the properties uses, open competition, etc.

Mortgage: equivalent to a lien. A mortgage is an enforceable contract which allows for the transfer of title to real property on a conditional basis and as a security for the payment of a debt or obligation (loan). A mortgage becomes void and is canceled out upon successfully meeting the requirements of the mortgage.

NAREB: abbreviation for National Association of Real Estate Boards

Net Income: the gross income minus the actual vacancies and expenses. The net income, or Net Operating Income (N.O.I.) minus the debt service (principle, interest, taxes, and insurance, or P.I.T.I.) equals the cash flow.

Net Lease and **Net, Net Lease:** This type of lease is usually found in commercial and industrial properties only where the tenant pays specified maintenance and operating expenses, such as repairs, painting, utility bills, etc., in addition to the rent. In a net, net lease, a variation of the above, the tenant also pays additional expenses, such as the mortgage payment and property taxes.

Net Listing: a formal agreement in which there is an expressly agreed-upon sale price below which the owner will not sell. The broker receives the excess above the net listing as his commission. A listing agreement with a variable commission ranging from zero on up.

Net Profit: the cash flow or the readily accessible cash which remains after all expenses and charges have been deducted from the gross profit; synonymous with net income or net operating income

Note: a signed, legally enforceable agreement which acknowledges a debt and outlines the repayment schedule; synonymous with mortgage note and promissory note

Obsolescence: Usually a decline in value due to a lessened desirability or usefulness. The decline in value is typically a result of major social, economic, or fashion changes.

Offer: a signed written agreement to purchase real estate at a particular price and under particular circumstances. It is generally accompanied by an earnest money deposit to demonstrate genuine intentions. A signed acceptance by the seller can convert an offer into a binding contract if all of the essential conditions are met. To remain an offer rather than an enforceable contract (where you could easily lose your deposit), an offer should contain one or more "In lieu of . . ." statements, such as: "In lieu of acceptable financing . . . , In lieu of a formal appraisal . . . ," etc.

Open Listing: a listing which is the opposite of an exclusive listing. An open listing may be given to any number of agents without the obligation to compensate anyone except the party who actually completes the sale. The owner also reserves the right to sell the property himself without financial liability to the listing agent.

Option: a written agreement which grants the exclusive right to purchase or control the use of a specific piece of property during a stated period of time, and at a stated purchase price. Although there is a price on the option itself, there is no obligation on the part of the grantee to purchase the property. Options are most common in controlling an interest in a large tract of under-developed land with the intent or expectation of a zoning change which would substantially increase the property's value.

Over-Improvement: any improvement or total accumulation of improvements which exceeds the appraisor's concept of "highest and best use" for a particular site. Example: improving a home to the $100,000 level in a neighborhood of $50,000 homes will make the property unmarketable at that price. The term generally implies the owner would not be able to get a comparable return on the investment upon the sale of the property.

Percentage Lease: generally a lease on business property in which the rental is determined as a percentage of the gross income and usually includes provisions for a minimum rental

Personality: all material items and goods which are not a part of the real estate. All property is personalty, realty, or a combination of the two.

Prepayment Penalty: During times of high-interest rates, lenders frequently gouge for additional profits by including a prepayment penalty clause in a mortgage agreement to make it virtually prohibitive to refinance the loan down to a lower rate of interest at any time in the future when the rate would invariably decline. Such penalties are never written into the mortgage agreements when the rates are low because the lender would be delighted to refinance the loan at higher rates.

Property: the legal right or interest which one possesses in lands and chattels to the exclusion of all others

Purchase Money Mortgage: a mortgage which is given to the seller by the buyer as part (usually a down payment) or all of the purchase price of the property. In the event of foreclosure of such a mortgage, the mortgagee (seller) is not entitled to a deficiency judgment.

Quiet Enjoyment: the right of an owner or tenant to utilize property without interference of possession

Quiet Title: a formal court action which establishes legal title and removes a cloud on the title

Real Estate: the land and all improvements or objects which are attached to the land, with the intent that those objects should pass with title to the land; synonymous with real property and distinguished from personal property or chattel property

Recission of Contract: the cancellation or annulling of a contract for cause by mutual consent of the parties or by court order

Recording: the act of formally recording or registering a new conveyance of real estate with the appropriate county office. Although not necessarily required, the recording of any change in the title to real property mainly protects the grantee (buyer) and provides constructive notice to the world that a change has occurred. Recording prevents a seller from selling the same parcel to different buyers without the buyers' mutual knowledge.

Redemption: the legal right of a property owner to redeem his or her property within a statutory period of time after a foreclosure sale.

The unlikely but not impossible condition is that all debts, expenses, and charges, including interest to date, must be paid.

Rent Schedule: an itemized listing of the scheduled (expected) rent per unit and the term of the lease per unit; distinguished from the actual rent which includes the vacancy factors by history

Replacement Cost: an appraiser's concept which refers to the current estimated cost of new construction per square foot. This shorthand appraisal technique is frequently used by insurance salespersons in establishing and updating fire insurance coverage.

Restrictive Covenant: a clause in a deed limiting the use of property conveyed for a certain period of time

Rights of Ownership: Ownership of real estate implies the right of possession, enjoyment, control, and disposition (*cf.* Quiet Enjoyment).

Second Mortgage: a lien or claim on real property which is subordinated to that of the first mortgage. A second mortgage takes precedence immediately after all first-mortgage claims have been settled, irregardless of other indebtedness or intervening liens. It is also referred to as a junior mortgage, or purchase-money mortgage.

Separate Property: any property owned by a husband and wife which is not community property and acquired by either spouse before marriage or by gift or devise after marriage

Statute of Frauds: All contracts pertaining to real estate must be in writing in order to be enforceable.

Straight-Line Depreciation: When used with income-producing properties, this refers to the establishment of an appropriate or reasonable number of "years' life" remaining in the property and the 100% depreciation of the purchase price (without the land) over that established period of years and on a non-declining balance. Example: on 20 years' life, deduct 5% from the balance each year; for 15 years' life, deduct .067% from the balance each year.

Syndicate: a group of investors formed for the purpose of buying and owning property for the mutual advantage of its members. Syndications are frequently, but not necessarily, set up on a general and limited partnership basis.

Tax: a charge, usually pecuniary, assessed against persons or property for public purposes

Tax Liens: Whenever the owner of real property is delinquent in paying his property taxes, the local taxing authority can initiate a lien or claim against the property which must be settled within certain time frames, or the cumbersome foreclosure process will be implemented.

Tax Shelter: a legitimate means which provides for the reduction, deferral, or elimination of a tax due without the expenditure of money. The potential for legitimately deferring some taxes is the major incentive for assuming the "risks" associated with investment properties. Ultimately, taxes must be paid at a capital gains rate on all profits after sale minus expenses and minus the depreciation which has already been claimed.

Tenancy at Sufferance: one who originally had possession by lawful title and who continues to maintain possession without any title at all. Also, this could refer to a situation in which one maintained possession of real property after the expiration of his lease.

Tenancy at Will: authorization to use or occupy property at the discretion of the owner. The rental agreement tends to be an oral lease. The tenant or landlord may cancel the lease at any time with written notice equal to one rental payment period.

Tenancy in Common: ownership by two or more persons who may or may not be related. Each person possesses a share of the total, which may or may not be equal. There are no rights of survivorship.

Title: the legally recognized verification of ownership of real property

Title Insurance: an insurance policy which is obtained by the purchaser of real property to indemnify the new owner against loss if the title is later found to be imperfect

Torrens System: a system of registering title records as provided by state law

Trust Deed: a conveyance of real estate to a trustee (third party) to be held for the benefit of a beneficiary and to be delivered upon repayment of a loan made to the grantor

Warranty Deed: a deed used to convey real property in which the grantor warrants or guarantees that he is the legal owner, can lawfully sell the property, and will protect the grantee against the claims of all other persons

Wrap-Around Mortgage: a second mortgage which is virtually indistinguishable from the first mortgage—*i.e.,* it is in effect "wrapped around" the first mortgage. The lender merely collects enough to satisfy the first and second mortgages as a single payment. The incentive or "sweetener" to the lender is that both the first and second mortgages are paid at the interest rate of the second mortgage even though the rate on the assumed first mortgage is probably less.

Yield: the annual percentage rate of return on an investment. A "total" yield can be determined only after an investor has completely exited from a property. Total yield includes annual cash flow, equity gain, tax-sheltered dollars, and profits from sale (appreciation, inflation, etc.) divided back over the life of the investment.

Zoning: municipal ordinances which are approved at the local government level for the purpose of limiting the use of property in specific areas. Slow, evolutionary changes in zoning requirements are a major basis for profit in real estate investment.

Index

Acceleration clause 126
Acknowledgement 123
Acquisition 5, 38
Acreage 110
Active management 41
Adequate heating and plumbing 151
Adjusted sales profit 186
Adversary relationship 138
Aging process 50
Agricultural property 31
Allocation 89
Allowable depreciation 37
Amenities 47, 51, 56, 74, 89, 139
American Dream 30
Amortization 76
Ample parking 74
Annual interest rates 126
Annual Property Operating Data 80, 84
Anticipatory maintenance 161
Anti-discrimination laws 151
Antiques 22
Apartment managers 50
Apartment Owner's Associations 151
Apartment units 47
Appraisal fees 126
Appraisal methods 77

Appraisers 98
Appreciation 39, 89, 183
Architectural barriers 74, 154
Articles of Incorporation 59
Asking price 103
Assaults 51
Assessed valuation 111
Assessment 80
Attorneys 53
Attractive furnishings 74
Audits 11

Baby-boom population 50
Balloon payment 181
Bank loan 117
Bankruptcy 24, 68
Bargain properties 110
Basic shelter 151
Basis 4, 38, 76
Benefits of ownership 96
Boundaries 109
Boundary disputes 109
Brinksmanship 172
Builder's replacement costs 98
Building code violations 151
Building inspectors 151
Building site costs 78
Building-sitter 49, 54
Buyer's aspiration 96
Buyer's market 33

Capital gains tax   5, 13, 82, 121, 127, 134
Capitalization rates (CAP rate)   84, 94
Carpentry   46
Carpet cleaning   45
Cash flow   4, 6, 183
Cash out   37, 112, 181
Caveat Emptor   37, 152, 167
Certificate Savings Program   66
Certified mail   158
Certified public accountants   32, 53
Certified True Income & Expense Statement   84
Chamber of Commerce   75, 106
Changing consumer preferences   72
Changing economic conditions   173
Checklists   98
Chronic delinquent   155
City-county right of way   110
Civil lawsuits   56
Civil rights   146, 154
Cleaning contractors   45
Cleaning fee   166
Closing cost   111
Collateral   66, 127
Collection losses   49, 52, 140
College campus   107
Commercial noise   106
Commercial properties   67
Commercial tenant   68
Commitment   48
Commodities   38
Common elements   59
Community of investors   85
Comparable properties   104
Comparable sales   98
Competitive bids   45
Competitively overpriced   48
Component method of depreciation   14
Concentrated crime   107
Condition of sale   110

Condominium law   59
Condominiums   9, 50, 55, 58, 88
Condominium record plat   59
Conflict of interest   40
Conservative institutional lenders   94
Consumer-protection groups   156
Consideration   123
Contemporary tenants   156
Contracts   42, 122, 181
Contract equity   122, 128
Contract law   151
Contractual agreement   104
Conventional loan   112, 117, 121
Conversion   37
Conversion of equities   129
Cooperatives   50, 55, 59, 88, 131
Corporations   55, 63
Cosmetic improvements   91
Cosmetic landscaping   36
Creation of wealth   27, 38
Creative landscaping   174
Creative sale   10
Creative refinancing   129, 132
Creatively advertise   56
Credit union   117
Current market equity   9, 38
Current market value   80
Custom built   88
Customer Service   107

Deadbeat   150
Deadbolts   51
Declining balance depreciation   13
Defective notice   158
Defects of appearance   162
Deferred capital gains taxes   186
Deferred maintenance   5, 20, 69, 161
Delinquent rent   152
Delinquent tenant   150
Demographic characteristics   21

Index 215

Dept. of Housing & Urban Development 24, 33, 119
Depreciated out 37
Depreciation 11, 71
Depreciation recapture 13
Direct approach 124
Direct sale 67, 180
Disability insurance 145
Discounts 9, 181
Discrimination against children 154
Dishonesty 73
Distressed property 135
Double declining balance 14
Double-digit inflation 22
Double-digit interest rates 123
Double mortgage payment 133
Drive by method 105

Earnest money 44
Easement problems 164
Earnest money agreement 5, 99, 114, 174
Economic boom periods 77
Economic life 11
Economic uncertainties 40
Economics of scarcity 90
Elderly 120
Electrical inspection 44
Encroachments 109
Energy crisis 78
Entranceways 91
Entrepreneurial businesses 38
Environmental concerns 64
Environmental law 79
Environmental restrictions 65
Equity growth 4, 8
Equity interest 66
Equity payoff 124-126
Exchange 10, 41, 58, 121, 179
Fair market price 66
Fair market value 80, 173
Fair weather investor 34
Falsified tenant records 164
Favorable tax treatment 112
Feasibility study 130

Fear of crime 107
Federally subsidized housing standards 158
Fee simple ownership 59
Fiduciary relationship 104, 193
Financial hardships 154
Financial independence 29
Financial penalties 131
Financial reference 57, 143
Financial trusts 55
Fire protection 78
First mortgage 127
F.H.A. 118, 133, 168
Floor plan 92
Forceable Entry & Detainer (F.E.D.) 150
Foreclosure 33, 122fn
Former tenants 149
Foundations 44, 168
Fuel 36

Garbage collection 165
Gasoline shortage 90
General partnerships 55
Gettel Method 95
G. I. loan 120
Gold bullion 1
Government insured loan 112
Government lands 62
Gross expenses 4
Gross income 77
Gross multiplier 94

Handicapped 120
Handyman special 162
Hard times 33
Heating bills 36
Hidden value 79
High interest rates 118
High percentage down payments 134
Highway noise 102
Hotels and motels 30
Housing discrimination 140

Illegal room sizes 29

Improper drainage 163
Income-generating problems 57
Income taxes 65
Incorporation 131
Indignant tenant 144
Individual investment goals 4
Industrial property 74
Industrial technology 74
Inflation 4, 21, 50, 64, 66, 111
Inflationary prices 105
Inheritance 52
"In lieu of" qualifiers 97
Inquiry forms 99
Installment credit 144
Installment payments 66
Installment sale 121, 127
Institutional banker 57
Insulation 152, 163
Insurance agents 32
Insurance companies 88
Insurance needs 57
Internal Revenue Service 11, 48, 57, 66, 77, 180, 187
Investor newsletters 93

Joint ownership 52
Joint tenancy 54
Journeyman's scale 44
Judgment 157
Judgment-free 157
Judgment by Stipulation 157

Lake Havasu City 62
Land sales contract 120
Landlord/landlady 42, 156
Landlord-tenant laws 40, 57
Landlord-tenant relations 149, 156
Landscaping 140
Landscaping contractors 45
Late fee 149
Late rental payments 149
Latex and enamel 169
Lawsuit 110, 152
Lease-back contract 75
Leases 49

Legal aid 51, 64, 156
Legal defenses 156
Legal description 107
Legal remedies 149
Legally binding contract 122
Leverage 4, 24, 187
Licensed appraiser 91
Like-kind investments 186
Limited partnerships 55, 131
Liquidity 4, 22, 160
Liquidated damages 181
List-price equity 9, 24, 53
Litigious tenants 159
Loan application fees 117
Location 89, 90
Long-term leases 67
Lot dimensions 107
Low-income 120
Lowry, Albert J. 29

Mail carriers 106
Maintenance 43, 54, 70
Maintenance-free 140, 160
Management 38, 64
Marginal properties 19
Market analysis 72
Meeting of the minds 179
Migration patterns 50
Mini-apartment complex 28
Minimum housing quality standards 151
Minimum livability standards 151
Misrepresentations 56
Mobility impaired persons 154
Money loser 101
Mortgage insurance 117, 126
Mortgage paper 38, 127, 182
Motels 71
Move-In Checklist 148
Multiple exchange 129
Multiple listings 103

Index

Municipal bonds 1
Municipal right of way 110
Mutual funds 38
Mutual savings banks 131

Negative cash flow 7, 63
Negotiation process 35
Neighborhoods 106
Net income 94
Net lease 69
Net, Net, Net lease 69
New construction costs 108
No money down 132
No vacancy sign 73
Non-depreciable lots 58
Non-resident investor 118
Novice investor 40, 63

Obnoxious pets 146
Off-season 36
Older tenants 50
One More Fool Theory 82
O.P.M. ("other people's money") 4, 24
Other people's dirt 161
Overall trends 93
Overfinanced 6, 19, 53, 131, 183
Overpriced property 81
Owner's fluff 102

Painting 46
Painting contractors 45
Partnerships 19
Passive income 127
Passive management 37
Peephole lenses 51
Permanent financing 130
Personal expectations 99
Perennials 176
Pest problems 164
Pets 176

Plans and specifications 130
Plot map 89
Plumbing inspection 44
Positive cash flow 58, 105
Positive selling features 102
Pre-payment penalties 126
Pre-sold units 133
Preventative maintenance 167
Pride of ownership 3, 39
Principle gain 8
Priority programs 132
Private contractors 43
Private financing 120
Professional deadbeats 140
Professional landscaping 175
Professional property management 43, 49
Professional speculators 62
Projected gross rental 4
Property appraisers 85
Property managers 32, 155
Property tax 82, 111
Property tax valuations 40
Proposition 13, 2, 83
Psychological needs 56
Public amenities 47
Public records 111
Public welfare 145
Purchasing power 22
Pyramid 53, 57, 133, 187

Random broker 57
Raw land 61
Ready, willing & able 173
Real estate brokers 32, 98
Real Estate Investment Trusts (R.E.I.T.'s) 31
Realistic National Marketing Institute 84
Real estate trusts 38
Recession 3, 33, 66
Recessionary economy 22

Record-keeping 42
Recreational needs 56
Recreational property 76-79
Refinance 10, 41, 110, 179, 182
Reminder notice 149
Renegotiated leases 69
Reno, Richard R. 129
Rent collection 54
Rent controls 83, 151, 153
Rent strike 139
Rental agreement 42
Rental applications 42, 141
Rental market 50
Rental properties 38
Rental rate 70
Replacement costs 88
Residential investment 48
Resident manager 49, 53
Retaliation 158
Ridiculous offers 102
Right to privacy 146
Risk 19, 42, 133
Risk factors 4
Rogers, Will 61
Rotted wood 163
Rule of Four-to-One 145
Rule of 30% 127, 180
Rural blight 30

Sales agents 103, 112
Savings & loan associations 131
Seasoned contracts 127, 182
Second mortgage 52
Secondary financing 123, 127
Section 8, Subsidy Tenants 120
Secure locks 74, 151
Security 56
Seller's fluff 103, 172
Seller's market 5, 113
Seller's rationale 82
Selling fee 64
Septic tank 44

Sexual orientation 154
Sheltered income 11
Shopping centers 31
Single-factor dimension 154
Single family dwelling 28
Slumlords 151
Small alligator 41, 52, 184
Small investor 32
Smoke alarms 140
Social Security 145
Special-interest groups 75
Specific performance 152
Speculation 63
Straight-line depreciation 12
Strong buyers 135
Structural problems 163
Subordinate mortgage 117
Subordination 132
Subsidized rents 153
Sufficient & lawful cause 157
Sum-of-the-year's digits 15
Survey fees 126
Survey records 110
Swamplands 89
Syndication 131

Tax assessment records 88, 107
Tax bracket 13, 42, 113
Tax codes 21
Tax consequences 105
Tax-deferred exchange 38, 67, 185
Tax-exempt dollars 183
Tax-free life insurance payoff 134
Tax-free money 132
Tax rebellion 22, 153
Tax shelter 4, 11, 64
Tenancy by the Entirety 55
Tenancy in Common 55
Tenants 8, 29
Tenant concerns 48

Tenant eviction 157
Tenant organizations 57
Tenant rights 150
Tenant's rental history 146
Tenant selection 140, 143
Tenant stability 67
Tenant turnover 153
Terms 5
Test of Reasonableness 11
Thin equities 9, 187
Thrift institutions 121
Timing 101
Title companies 107
Titled interest 66
Title records 92
Total square footage 108
Total yield 4, 16, 58, 62
Tourists 72
Trading up 121
True market value 112
Twenty-four Hour Notice 149

Undeveloped land 64
Union shops 43
Unlawful discrimination 158
Unique building designs 75
Unusable space 108
Upside potential 105
Urban blight 30

Usable water 65
Utilities 94
Utility companies 106

Vacancy rates 33
Vacant land 66
Vandalism 78
Verifiable credit references 68
Veteran's Administration 118, 132, 168
View property 89
Visitor parking area 140
Visual appeal 89, 90
Visual impression 108
Visual inspection 101

Waste disposal 65
Wear and tear 148
Wrap-around mortgage 123
Written application 140

Years life 12
Yield 127
Young tenants 51

Zero-vacancy factor 105
Zoning 21, 40, 64, 79
Zoning changes 112
Zoning restrictions 164